Study Guide to Accompany
Newman and Newman's
DEVELOPMENT THROUGH LIFE
A Psychosocial Approach

7TH EDITION

Barbara M. Newman
The Ohio State University

Philip R. Newman

Laura Landry-Meyer
The Ohio State University

Brenda J. Lohman
The Ohio State University

Mary C. Myers
The Ohio State University

Brooks/Cole • Wadsworth

I(T)P®   An International Thomson Publishing Company

Pacific Grove • Albany • Belmont • Bonn • Boston • Cincinnati • Detroit • Johannesburg • London
Madrid • Melbourne • Mexico City • New York • Paris • Singapore • Tokyo • Toronto • Washington

Senior Assistant Editor: *Faith B. Stoddard*
Editorial Assistant: *Stephanie M. Andersen*
Production Coordinator: *Dorothy Bell*
Cover Design: *Roy R. Neuhaus*
Printing and Binding: *Patterson Printing*

COPYRIGHT © 1999 by Wadsworth Publishing Company
A division of International Thomson Publishing Inc.
I(T)P   The ITP logo is a registered trademark used herein under license.

Cover Art: Pablo Picasso, *Colombe Bleue avec Fleurs* 1957
© 1999 Estate of Pablo Picasso/Artists Rights Society (ARS), New York
Le Visage de la Paix by Pablo Picasso (1881-1973)
Private Collection/Bridgeman Art Library, London/New York

For more information, contact:

WADSWORTH PUBLISHING COMPANY
10 Davis Drive
Belmont, CA 94002
USA

International Thomson Editores
Seneca 53
Col. Polanco
11560 México, D. F., México

International Thomson Publishing Europe
Berkshire House 168-173
High Holborn
London WC1V 7AA
England

International Thomson Publishing GmbH
Königswinterer Strasse 418
53227 Bonn
Germany

Thomas Nelson Australia
102 Dodds Street
South Melbourne, 3205
Victoria, Australia

International Thomson Publishing Asia
60 Albert Street
#15-01 Albert Complex
Singapore 189969

Nelson Canada
1120 Birchmount Road
Scarborough, Ontario
Canada M1K 5G4

International Thomson Publishing Japan
Hirakawacho Kyowa Building, 3F
2-2-1 Hirakawacho
Chiyoda-ku, Tokyo 102
Japan

All rights reserved. No part of this work may be reproduced, stored in a retrieval system, or transcribed, in any form or by any means—electronic, mechanical, photocopying, recording, or otherwise—without the prior written permission of the publisher, Brooks/Cole Publishing Company, Pacific Grove, California 93950.

Printed in the United States of America
10 9 8 7 6 5 4 3 2 1
ISBN 0-534-35963-9

PREFACE

To the Student:

There are many ways to approach studying for your course in human development depending upon your learning style, your motivation, your background, and the course objectives. The purpose of this Study Guide is to provide a variety of strategies for study, and to help you focus on key ideas as you read and review. Research has demonstrated that you will improve your mastery of academic material and your test performance if you actively engage the material in addition to reading and listening to lectures. Participate in class discussion, meet with other students to talk about your ideas, try to translate concepts into your own words and relate them to your own observations or experiences, look for the links among topics and trace patterns or themes across life stages. The more you use the ideas and link them with other information, the more they become a meaningful part of your knowledge base.

The Study Guide is not intended to be a substitute for reading the text and other assigned readings suggested by your instructor. The text is not presented in brief here. Rather, we have developed this guide in order to focus your attention on the organization, basic concepts, and underlying issues of each chapter. In addition, we have provided a set of pre-test and post-test questions for each chapter to help strengthen your test-taking skills and to help assess improvement in your mastery of the concepts.

Each chapter of the Study Guide follows the same eight-step organization. If you follow these steps, you will have a solid grasp of important information in the text and you will find that the concepts become more fully integrated into the way you think and talk about development.

Step One. Before reading the chapter, review the chapter outline. This gives you a clear idea of the main topics to be covered in the chapter and how they are related to one another.

Step Two. Review the chapter objectives. These statements summarize the main goals of each chapter and alert you to important themes.

Step Three. Before reading the chapter, take the 10-item pre-test. This exercise will focus your attention on important ideas. It will also help you appreciate how much additional information you can gain by reading the text. The Answer Key for the pre-test is at the back of the Study Guide. Give yourself a score on the pre-test before going on to read the chapter. Use the page numbers cited with each question to find information related to specific questions. The topics covered in the pre-test and the post-test are not exhaustive. You should expect to be examined over a much wider range of information than is presented in the pre- and post-tests. However, these tests will give you a starting point for guiding your reading and assessing your growth in knowledge.

Step Four. Read the chapter. As you read, use the chapter objectives and the topics covered in the pre-test to make sure that you are paying attention to main ideas.

Step Five. Review basic concepts by matching each important term with its definition. It is good practice to work both from words to their definitions, and from definitions to the words. This exercise will strengthen you ability to use new vocabulary and to differentiate similar concepts. The list does not include all the terms introduced in each chapter. It focuses on words that may be unfamiliar or that may be used in a specific sense in the chapter. The correct answers for the matching questions are provided in the Answer Key at the end of the Study Guide. As you read the chapter, be sure to consider all the words that are in bold face. These terms are in the glossary and are defined again there.

Step Six. Answer the focusing questions. These questions are intended to help you summarize basic ideas from the text and to develop new ideas based on what you have read. Use your own words to answer these questions. The more easily you can explain ideas in your own terms, the more confident you can be that you understand them.

Step Seven. Take the 10-item post-test. The post-test often includes questions that have more specific information than that required in the pre-test. The Answer Key for the post-test is provided at the end of the Study Guide. Be sure to go back and reread the material related to any questions you missed or questions you felt uncertain about. The difference between your pre-test and your post-test scores will give you some idea of the effectiveness of your study strategies.

Another helpful tactic is to make up your own multiple choice questions about topics covered in the text. This forces you to break down ideas and information into very specific elements and reframe those elements into questions.

Step Eight. Suggestions for further observation and study are offered as a last step. We hope that you will enrich the meaning of the course by linking main ideas to your own personal observations, experiences, and additional reading. In each chapter, questions are raised about the application of human development research and theory to specific life experiences and challenges. The suggestions offered in the last section of each Study Guide chapter draw your attention to these issues in an attempt to build a richer context for your current learning and future study.

TABLE OF CONTENTS

Chapter One	The Development Through Life Perspective	1
Chapter Two	Psychosocial Theory	10
Chapter Three	Major Theories for Understanding Human Development	18
Chapter Four	The Period of Pregnancy and Prenatal Development	26
Chapter Five	Infancy (Birth to 2 years)	36
Chapter Six	Toddlerhood (Years 2 and 3)	46
Chapter Seven	Early School Age (4 to 6 years)	55
Chapter Eight	Middle Childhood (6 to 12 years)	64
Chapter Nine	Early Adolescence (12 to 18 years)	73
Chapter Ten	Later Adolescence (18 to 24 years)	82
Chapter Eleven	Early Adulthood (24 to 34 years)	91
Chapter Twelve	Middle Adulthood (34 to 60 years)	101
Chapter Thirteen	Later Adulthood (60 to 75 years)	111
Chapter Fourteen	Very Old Age (75 until Death)	120
Answer Key		128

CHAPTER ONE

The Development Through Life Perspective

Step One: Review the Chapter Outline

Assumptions of the Text
A Psychosocial Approach: The Interaction of the Biological, Psychological, and Societal Systems
    The Biological System
    The Psychological System
    The Societal System
        The Psychosocial Impact of Poverty
    Overview of the Psychosocial Approach
The Scientific Process
    Scientific Observation
    Research Design
    Selecting a Sample
        Random Samples
        Stratified Samples
        Matched Groups
        Volunteer Samples
        Strengths and Weaknesses of Approaches to Sampling
    Research Methods
        Observation
        Case Study
        Interviews
        Surveys and Tests
        Experimentation
    Designs for Studying Development
        Retrospective Studies
        Cross-sectional Studies
        Longitudinal Studies
        Cohort Sequential Studies
    Evaluating Existing Research
    Ethics
The Life Span
Chapter Summary
End of Chapter Case

Step Two: Review the Chapter Objectives

1.1 To introduce the basic assumptions that underlie the organization and focus of the text.
1.2 To introduce the psychosocial approach, including the interrelationships among the biological, psychological, and societal systems.
1.3 To define the scientific process and review basic research principles for the study of human development.
1.4 To consider the ethical guidelines that should be used in conducting research with human subjects.
1.5 To note historical changes in life expectancy and examine the implications of these changes for the study of development over the life span.

Step Three: Take the Pre-Test

Answer these questions before you read the chapter. The pages where material is discussed are indicated in the parentheses after each question. Use your performance as a guide to areas where you need to read especially carefully. The Answer Key for the pre-test can be found at the end of the study guide.

1. When is growth and change likely to occur? (p. 3)
   a. in infancy
   b. in adolescence.
   c. in early adulthood
   d. at every period of life.

2. What are the three major systems that interact to produce human experience? (p. 3)
   a. biological, psychological, and societal systems
   b. democratic, capitalist, and socialist systems
   c. fantasy, reasoning, and the unconscious
   d. respiratory, circulatory, and metabolic systems

3. Which of the following is most likely to bring about change in the biological system? (pp. 3-4)
   a. use of drugs
   b. entry into new roles
   c. movement from one culture to the next
   d. age graded expectations

4. Which of the following is most likely to bring about change in the psychological system? (pp. 4-5)
   a. disease
   b. environmental toxins
   c. education
   d. accidents

5. Which of the following is most likely to bring about change in the societal system? (pp. 4-5)
   a. genetic factors
   b. insight
   c. nutrition
   d. entry into new roles

6. What are three characteristics of scientific observation? (pp. 10-11)
   a. systematic, objective, and repeatable
   b. interview, experimentation, and case study
   c. random, stratified, and volunteer
   d. biological, psychological, and societal

7. What is naturalistic observation? (p. 13)
   a. Monitoring and recording behavior in a laboratory setting.
   b. Monitoring and recording behavior where it normally takes place.
   c. Observing and recording behaviors in nature, that is in oceans, forests, prairies, etc.
   d. Observing and recording innate rather than learned behaviors.

8. If you carried out an in-depth analysis of a single person or a family, gathering data from many sources, you would be using which of the following research methods? (p. 15)
   a. experimentation
   b. survey research
   c. naturalistic observation
   d. case study

9. What is a cross-sectional research study? (p. 22)
   a. A study that uses only naturalistic observation as a source of data.
   b. A study that follows the same people over time.
   c. A study that compares different groups of people at one time.
   d. A study that uses only surveys as a source of data, not observation or interviews.

10. In what way has the life expectancy at birth changed in the U. S. over this century? (pp. 24-25)
    a. It has increased by about 50% for both men and women.
    b. It has remained steady for men, but increased for women.
    c. It has remained steady for women, but increased for men.
    d. The average life expectancy has remained the same, but people die of new causes than they did in the past.

Step Four: Read Chapter 1: The Development Through Life Perspective

Step Five: Review Basic Concepts By Matching Each Term and its Definition

a.	biological system	b.	psychological system
c.	societal system	d.	psychosocial approach
e.	scientific process	f.	research design
g.	ethics	h.	life expectancy
i.	operational definition	j.	research methods

1. ( ) The number of years of life, based on the average length of life for a given population.

2. ( ) All the processes necessary for thinking and reasoning.

3. ( ) All the processes necessary for the functioning of the biological organism.

4. ( ) Principles of morality that guide conduct.

5. ( ) A theoretical framework for studying human development that emphasizes the interaction of the biological, psychological, and societal systems over the lifespan.

6. ( ) All the processes through which a person becomes integrated into society.

7. ( ) The various techniques and strategies used for gathering data.

8. ( ) The components of a research project including the sample, methods of gathering data, decisions about how often data will be gathered, and use of statistical techniques to analyze the data.

9. ( ) A method for systematically building a body of information and evaluating the accuracy of that information.

10. ( ) The translation of an abstract concept into a procedure that is observable and measurable.

Step Six: Answer the Focusing Questions

1. What are the major assumptions underlying the organization and focus of the textbook? (p. 3)

2. What are two examples of ways that the psychological system is influenced by the biological system? (pp. 3-5)

3. What are two examples of ways that the psychological system is influenced by the societal system? (pp. 3-5)

4. What are the biological, psychological, and societal aspects of poverty? (pp. 6-7)

5. What is the relationship between theory and research in the scientific process? (pp. 8-10)

6. What are the strengths and weaknesses of each of the research methods discussed in the text? (pp. 13-21)

7. What changes have occurred in the life expectancy over this century? What are some explanations for these changes? What might account for the projected shrinking of differences in life expectancy for men and women in the next ten years? (pp. 25-28)

Step Seven: Take the Post-Test

1. Which of the following statements best reflects the assumptions of the text? (p.3)
   a. Personality is fixed by age 6.
   b. New psychosocial development occurs at every life stage.
   c. Psychosocial development is complete once identity formation occurs.
   d. Development in adulthood occurs in the societal system only.

2. Which system includes all the mental processes central to the person's ability to make meaning of experiences and take action? (p. 4)
   a. The biological system
   b. The psychological system
   c. The societal system
   d. The scientific system

3. Which parts of the scientific process allow us to determine whether a theory is correct? (pp. 8-10)
   a. constructing the theory
   b. operationalizing the theory
   c. testing the theory and evaluating the results
   d. accepting the theory

4. Scientific observation differs from personal observation in that it aims to be _____. (pp. 10-11)
   a. repeatable, immediate, and subjective
   b. objective, random, and isolated
   c. subjective, repeatable, and systematic
   d. objective, repeatable, and systematic

5. Although a scholar may believe that his or her research findings are relevant to a wide group of people, the generalizability of the findings is usually limited to _____. (p. 11)
   a. The sample and the population from which the sample is drawn.
   b. The people living in the researcher's city.
   c. The people who participated in the study.
   d. People of the same race and sex as the sample.

6. Which research method suffers from the difficulty in achieving interobserver reliability? (p. 15)
   a. case study
   b. observation
   c. interview
   d. surveys/tests

7. Which of the following is NOT an advantage of the experimental method? (pp. 20-21)
   a. It captures what happens naturally in the person's life settings.
   b. It permits the researcher to isolate and control specific variables.
   c. It allows one to compare the impact of specific treatments.
   d. It leads to statements about causal relationships.

8. Why is the cohort sequential design an **improvement** over the cross-sectional design? (pp. 22-23)
   a. It allows one to study people of different ages at the same time.
   b. It follows the same individuals over repeated observations across time.
   c. It takes a lot longer to complete the cohort sequential research design.
   d. It encourages participants to think back about earlier periods in their life.

9. Dr. Good is on a panel reviewing research proposals. He looks at each proposal and asks, "Is the stress or pain inflicted on participants associated with this procedure worth the benefit to society from the potential results?" This is an example of which of the following scientific concerns? (pp. 23-24)
   a. operational definition
   b. theoretical framework
   c. objectivity
   d. ethics

10. Which statement about life expectancy for people who are 80 years old is accurate? (p. 25)
    a. People who were 80 in 1994 could expect to live to 82.
    b. People who were 80 at the turn of the century could expect to live to 82.
    c. There has been over a 50% increase in the life expectancy of people who are 80 from 1900 to the present.
    d. Once people are 80, it is impossible to predict their life expectancy.

After completing the post-test, compare your score with your performance on the pre-test. Can you identify areas where significant new learning has taken place? If you still have questions about some sections of the chapter, read them again. Check the glossary. You may want to discuss some of your questions with your instructor.

Step Eight: Suggestions for Further Observation and Study

1. Think about the impact of poverty in the life of Patrick Jonathan Carmichael. What might be some resources that helped him cope with these challenges? Imagine that you live for 100 years; what will be the most important personal resources you will draw upon to remain positive and hopeful over your lifetime?

2. Consider the case of Rose at the end of the chapter. How do the biological, psychological, and societal systems interact in her case? Think of your own example of someone who is experiencing significant conflict. How do the three systems interact in that case?

3. Start with a puzzling observation, something of interest to you. Think of how you might study this question using each of the research methods discussed in the text: observation, case study, interview, surveys/tests, and experimentation. Which approach seems best suited to the topic you have in mind?

4. Use the information at the end of Chapter 1, including Table 1.4, to project your life expectancy. What changes would you be willing to make in your lifestyle to increase your chances of living a long life?

CHAPTER TWO

Psychosocial Theory

Step One: Review the Chapter Outline

What Is a Theory?
The Rationale for Emphasizing Psychosocial Theory
Basic Concepts of Psychosocial Theory
    Stages of Development
    Developmental Tasks
    Psychosocial Crisis
        A Typical Psychosocial Crisis
        Psychosocial Crises of the Life Stages
    The Central Process for Resolving the Psychosocial Crisis
    Radius of Significant Relationships
        Contexts of Development
    Coping Behavior
        Prime Adaptive Ego Qualities
        Core Pathologies
Evaluation of Psychosocial Theory
    Strengths
    Weaknesses
    A Recap of Psychosocial Theory
Chapter Summary
End of Chapter Case

Step Two: Review the Chapter Objectives

2.1   To define the concept of theory and explain how one makes use of theory to increase understanding.
2.2   To define the six basic concepts of psychosocial theory.
2.3   To demonstrate how the concepts of psychosocial theory contribute to an analysis of basic processes that foster or inhibit development over the lifespan.
2.4   To evaluate psychosocial theory, pointing out its strengths and weaknesses.

Step Three: Take the Pre-Test

Answer these questions before you read the chapter. The pages where material is discussed are indicated in the parentheses after each question. Use your performance as a guide to areas where you need to read especially carefully. The Answer Key for the pre-test can be found at the end of the study guide.

1. A _____ is a logical system of concepts that provides a framework for organizing and interpreting observations. (p. 32)
   a. theory
   b. variable
   c. symbol
   d. correlation

2. The guiding premises underlying the logic of a theory are its _____. (p. 33)
   a. predictions
   b. assumptions
   c. variables
   d. applications

3. Which of the following best describes the range of applicability for psychosocial theory? (pp. 33-34)
   a. changes in unconscious processes during childhood
   b. patterns of psychological and social change and growth over the life course
   c. how habits are created and sustained in adulthood
   d. how logical thinking changes from infancy through adolescence

4. Psychosocial theory focuses on the interaction between individual needs and abilities, and which of the following? (p.34)
   a. a college education
   b. experiences in other cultures
   c. social expectations and demands
   d. logical reasoning

5. Which of the following is NOT a central concept of psychosocial theory? (p. 35)
   a. stages of development
   b. coping
   c. psychosocial crises
   d. functional autonomy of motives

6. A _____ is a period of life that is characterized by a specific underlying organization. (p. 35)
   a. psychosocial stage
   b. developmental task
   c. psychosocial crisis
   d. core pathology

7. Which is the best definition of developmental tasks? (p. 39)
   a. chores to do around the house
   b. rituals that are performed at various ages
   c. planning for a goal and reaching that goal
   d. skills and competencies that contribute to increased mastery

8. Which of the following terms refers to the tension between the person's competencies at the beginning of a stage and social expectations for how one ought to function at that period of life? (p. 43)
   a. psychosocial theory
   b. psychosocial crisis
   c. psychosocial environment
   d. psychosocial stage

9. The ability to gather and process new information is a key element of _____. (pp. 49-50).
   a. coping behavior
   b. defensive behavior
   c. core pathologies
   d. life crises

10. What is one weakness of psychosocial theory? (pp. 52-54)
    a. It focuses on childhood rather than adulthood.
    b. It hypothesizes a specific direction for healthy growth at each life stage.
    c. The basic concepts are abstract and difficult to measure.
    d. The psychosocial crisis is not the same from one stage to the next.

Step Four: Read Chapter 2: Psychosocial Theory

Step Five: Review Basic Concepts By Matching Each Term and Its Definition

a.	theory	b.	psychosocial theory
c.	developmental stage	d.	developmental tasks
e.	coping	f.	central process
g.	psychosocial crisis	h.	radius of significant relationships
i.	core pathologies	j.	prime adaptive ego qualities

1. ( ) A theory of human development which proposes that cognitive, emotional, and social growth are a product of the interaction between social expectations at each life stage and the competencies people bring to each life challenge.

2. ( ) A predictable tension between personal competencies and social expectations.

Chapter 2

3. ( ) Mental states that emerge in the positive resolution of each psychosocial crisis which form a basic orientation toward the interpretation of life experiences.

4. ( ) Active efforts to keep stress at a manageable level.

5. ( ) Skills and competence that are acquired at each stage of development.

6. ( ) Destructive forces that result from severe, negative resolutions of each psychosocial crisis.

7. ( ) The predominant mechanism through which a psychosocial crisis is resolved.

8. ( ) A period of life that is characterized by some underlying organization or emphasis.

9. ( ) The range of important interpersonal bonds through which social expectations reach the person and from which the person derives essential social support.

10. ( ) A logical system of concepts that provides a framework for organizing and understanding observations.

Step Six: Answer the Focusing Questions

1. What is meant when one refers to a theory's **range of applicability**? What is the range of applicability of psychosocial theory? (p. 33)

   _____
   _____
   _____
   _____

2. What four issues should a theory of human development address? How does psychosocial theory address these issues? (pp. 33-51)

   _____
   _____
   _____
   _____

3. Using Figure 2.1 on page 35, explain how each of the main concepts of psychosocial theory operates to produce development at each stage of life. (pp. 35-51)

_____
_____
_____
_____

4. In your own words, explain three strengths and three weaknesses of psychosocial theory. (pp. 52-54)

_____
_____
_____
_____

Step Seven: Take the Post-Test

1. One of the central functions of a _____ is to describe unobservable mechanisms or structures and relate them to one another and to observable events. (p. 32)
   a. psychosocial crisis
   b. developmental task
   c. theory
   d. coping strategy

2. Which of the following is an assumption of psychosocial theory? (pp. 33-34, 55)
   a. At every stage of life, individuals contribute to their own development.
   b. The direction of growth follows a genetically guided course that is impervious to cultural influences.
   c. Development is shaped largely through experiences in the first six years of life.
   d. The combination of differences among cultures and individual differences make it impossible to speak of patterns of development.

3. According to psychosocial theory, development occurs as a result of which of the following processes? (p. 34)
   a. reinforcements and punishments
   b. modeling and imitation
   c. the interaction between individual needs and abilities, and social expectations and demands
   d. the modification of boundaries and subsystems as a result of feedback and adaptive self-regulation

4. Which of the following is NOT a characteristic of developmental stages in psychosocial theory? (pp. 35-39)
   a. Each new stage incorporates gains made in earlier stages.
   b. The stages reflect a biologically based plan for the nature and direction and growth.
   c. Each new stage brings a qualitatively new approach for understanding oneself and others.
   d. Once a stage is passed, there is no way to review or reinterpret events from that stage.

5. Which of the following illustrates the idea of a sensitive period? (p. 40)
   a. Marla is turning five and her feelings are easily hurt if you criticize her behavior.
   b. Language is most readily learned during the first four years of life; afterward it becomes more difficult to acquire language skills.
   c. At age 65, Fred is experiencing hearing loss. He has a hard time understanding what people are saying to him, but he doesn't want to have hearing aids because to him they are a sign of aging.
   d. Each stage of life has some characteristics that differentiate it from the one before and the one after.

6. Which of the following is the best definition of the term psychosocial crisis? (pp. 43-44).
   a. the tension state caused by discrepancies between individual competencies at the beginning of a stage and society's expectations for new levels of functioning
   b. the loss of reality testing abilities as a result of a severe trauma
   c. mental states that emerge at each stage which create a basically positive orientation toward the interpretation of life experiences
   d. an interpersonal bond that can be maintained or broken across stages of life

7. At each stage of development, the person has the capacity to engage in a changing network of meaningful social relationships. What is this called? (p. 47)
   a. prime adaptive ego quality
   b. coping
   c. radius of significant relationships
   d. ethnicity

8. Which of the following are discussed as the three primary social contexts for development? (pp. 47-49)
   a. family, culture, and ethnic group
   b. school, work, and community
   c. home, neighborhood, and country
   d. friends, family, and work

9. After five years of marriage, Karen has recently divorced her husband. After a period of grief and withdrawal, Karen has decided to join a support group. She is taking classes at a community college to begin to focus on a career, and she has started a program of regular exercise which helps relieve stress and improve her feeling of confidence. Which concept best describes Karen's behaviors? (pp. 49-50)
   a. psychosocial stage of development
   b. coping
   c. prime adaptive ego qualities
   d. core pathologies

10. What does the text identify as a special strength of psychosocial theory? (p. 52)
    a. It highlights the dynamic interplay between individual development and culture.
    b. The concepts of the theory are difficult to translate into objective measures, so it is not easily distorted by research.
    c. The theory gives special attention to infancy and toddlerhood as key periods of development.
    d. The stages of development are patterned after non-Western theories of self and society.

After completing the post-test, compare your score with your performance on the pre-test. Can you identify areas where significant new learning has taken place? If you still have questions about some sections of the chapter, read them again. Check the glossary. You may want to discuss some of your questions with your instructor.

Step Eight: Suggestions for Further Observation and Study

1. Read more about Erik Erikson and his works:
   Coles, R. (1970). Erik H. Erikson: The growth of his works. Boston: Atlantic-Little Brown.
   Erikson, E. H. (1963). Childhood and society. (2nd edition). New York: W. W. Norton.
   Gross, F. L., Jr. (1987). Introducing Erik Erikson: An invitation to his thinking. New York: University Press of America.
   Web Site: http://snycorva.cortland.edu/~andermd/erik/welcome.html to learn more regarding Erikson and Psychosocial Theory
2. Review the stages of development listed in Figure 2.3, page 38. What are some experiences that are unique to each age group? How does society treat individuals in each age that might suggest that they are members of a common stage of life?

3. Consider the various rings in the radius of significant relationships described in Figure 2.4, page 48. For each ring, list two or three ways that you are influenced by individuals in that sphere. As examples, individuals at each level might have unique expectations for your behavior, serve as sources of encouragement or support, or provide opportunities for new learning.

4. Using Table 2.7, identify your own life stage and consider your progress on the developmental tasks of the preceding stage, the current stage, and the following stage. How confident are you about your mastery of the issues in these three adjoining stages? How would you describe your resolution of the crises in these three stages? What kinds of experiences might help you move to a new level of mastery around the issues of your life stage?

CHAPTER THREE

Major Theories for Understanding Human Development

Step One: Review the Chapter Outline

The Theory of Evolution
    Implications for Human Development
    Links to Psychosocial Theory
Psychosexual Theory
    Implications for Human Development
    Links to Psychosocial Theory
Cognitive Developmental Theory
    Basic Concepts in Piaget's Theory
        Implications for Human Development
    Vygotsky's Concepts of Cognitive Development
        Implications for Human Development
    Links to Psychosocial Theory
Theories of Learning
    Classical Conditioning
        Implications for Human Development
    Operant Conditioning
        Implications for Human Development
    Social Learning
        Implications for Human Development
    Cognitive Behaviorism
        Implications for Human Development
    Summary of the Learning Theories
    Links to Psychosocial Theory
Cultural Theory
    Implications for Human Development
    Links to Psychosocial Theory
Social Role Theory
    Implications for Human Development
    Links to Psychosocial Theory
Systems Theory
    Implications for Human Development
    Links to Psychosocial Theory
Chapter Summary
End of Chapter Case

Step Two: Review the Chapter Objectives

3.1 To review the basic concepts of seven major theories that have guided research in the study of human development. These theories include: evolutionary theory; psychosexual theory; cognitive developmental theory, theories of learning, cultural theory; social role theory; and systems theory.

3.2 To examine the implications of each theory for the study of human development.

3.3 To clarify the links between each theory and psychosocial theory.

Step Three: Take the Pre-Test

Answer these questions before you read the chapter. The pages where material is discussed are indicated in the parentheses after each question. Use your performance as a guide to areas where you need to read especially carefully. The Answer Key for the pre-test can be found at the end of the study guide.

1. Which of the following terms from evolutionary theory refers to the process by which living organisms adapt to changing environmental conditions over long periods of time? (p. 62)
    a. uniformitarianism
    b. natural selection
    c. cultural determinism
    d. metacognition

2. Which of the following fields focuses on describing and comparing adaptive behaviors among various animal species? (p. 63)
    a. sociology
    b. anthropology
    c. ethology
    d. paleontology

3. According to psychosexual theory, what are the stages of development? (p. 66)
    a. oral, anal, latency, phallic, genital
    b. id, ego, superego
    c. unconscious, preconscious, conscious
    d. reaction formation, projection, and denial

4. What is one similarity between psychosexual theory and psychosocial theory? (p. 67)
   a. They both focus primarily on development up through age 6 as the critical time for change.
   b. They both emphasize the centrality of sexual impulses as the major area of conflict in development.
   c. They both view the middle childhood years as a time for consolidation, when little of importance occurs in personality development.
   d. They both describe changes in the development and capacity of the ego system.

5. A basic assumption of Piaget's theory of cognitive development is that the organism strives to achieve _____. (p. 68)
   a. equilibrium
   b. autonomy
   c. conservation
   d. object permanence

6. Vygotsky's view that cognition must be understood as an analysis of the person in activity in a setting is referred to as _____. (p. 70)
   a. optimism
   b. determinism
   c. contextualism
   d. discontinuity

7. According to the principles of classical conditioning, events that occur very close together in time come to have _____. (p. 72)
   a. different intensity
   b. different meaning
   c. similar intensity
   d. similar meaning

8. Which theory of learning emphasizes the impact of the cognitive structures such as expectations, plans, and goals on performance? (p. 77)
   a. classical conditioning
   b. cognitive behaviorism
   c. operant conditioning
   d. unconscious learning

9. Which of the following is an example of cultural continuity? (p. 79)
   a. Children take care of younger siblings and then grow up to take care of their own children.
   b. All children must learn the proper place and manners associated with elimination.
   c. Children are told not to fight, but at age 16 they are required to enlist in the army.
   d. Some societies restrict access to certain knowledge to a small group of "healers" or "medicine men/women."

10. Which of the following theories focuses on the processes and relationships among interconnected elements or organizations? (p. 83).
   a. psychosexual theory
   b. evolutionary theory
   c. systems theory
   d. cognitive behaviorism

Step Four: Read Chapter 3: Major Theories for Understanding Human Development

Step Five: Review Basic Concepts By Matching Each Term and Its Definition

a.	natural selection	b.	ethology
c.	psychosocial evolution	d.	unconscious
e.	ego	f.	equilibrium
g.	classical conditioning	h.	zone of proximal development
i.	operant conditioning	j.	vicarious reinforcement
k.	cognitive map	l.	cultural determinism
m.	role strain	n.	open systems

1. ( ) Psychological development is shaped by cultural expectations, resources, and challenges.

2. ( ) Structures that maintain their organization even though their parts are constantly changing.

3. ( ) The comparative study of unique adaptive behaviors that contribute to species survival.

4. ( ) The creation of new information and methods for passing that information from one generation to the next.

5. ( ) Learning that occurs when events take place close together in time and thus acquire a similar meaning.

6. ( ) A process that accounts for how species change in response to changing environmental conditions over long periods of time.

7. ( ) Reality oriented functions such as reasoning, remembering, and planning.

8. ( ) A balance in the organization of mental structures that provides the person with effective ways of interpreting experience and interacting with the environment.

9. ( )   A sense of overload that occurs when too many expectations are associated with one's roles.

10. ( )   The distance between the actual level of development and the level one can achieve when guided by a more capable teacher or peer.

11. ( )   Learning that is guided by observing the consequences of the behavior for others.

12. ( )   An area of mental functioning and a storehouse of wishes and drives of which one is unaware.

13. ( )   An internal mental representation of the learning environment.

14. ( )   Learning that emerges as a result of repetition and reinforcement.

Step Six: Answer the Focusing Questions

1. How are the concepts of evolutionary theory, which focus on species adaptation over long periods of time, related to the issues of human development within a single lifetime? (pp. 62-63)

   _____

   _____

   _____

2. Each of the seven theories places a slightly different emphasis on biological/hereditary factors and environmental factors in accounting for development. For example, evolutionary theory places almost all the emphasis on heredity and the transmission of genes from one generation to the next. For each theory, briefly state the role given to heredity and environment.

   _____

   _____

   _____

   _____

3. What do the learning theories, social role theory, and cultural theory have in common?

_____

_____

_____

_____

4. Of all the theories discussed in Chapter 3, which ones seem to be most closely related to psychosocial theory? What does psychosocial theory add that these theories do not provide?

_____

_____

_____

_____

Step Seven: Take the Post-Test

1. Which of the following theories argues for stages of development?
    a. psychosexual theory
    b. evolutionary theory
    c. classical conditioning
    d. social role theory

2. The reason that natural selection can contribute to species change is that species exhibit _____. (p. 63)
    a. habits
    b. social behavior
    c. child rearing skills
    d. variability

3. Which of the following is one of the important contributions of psychosexual theory to the study of human development? (p. 66)
   a. It emphasized the significant influence of childhood experiences on adult behavior.
   b. It pointed out the role of imitation as a process of learning.
   c. It clarified how children can be influenced by their parents' experiences in adjoining systems.
   d. It highlighted the new and vital changes in personality development that occur after adolescence.

4. In cognitive developmental theory, equilibrium is achieved through a process of _____. (p. 68)
   a. fixation
   b. adaptation
   c. conditioning
   d. rewards and punishments

5. Vygotsky argued that complex mental operations exist first in the social world and are then internalized. He described this as movement from the _____ to the _____. (pp. 70-71)
   a. ego, superego
   b. intermental, intramental
   c. model, child
   d. microsystem, mesosystem

6. Which of the following is an example of a negative reinforcer? (pp. 73-74)
   a. A mother smiles, the baby smiles, and the mother smiles again.
   b. A baby cries, the mother shouts at the baby, the baby cries louder; the next time the baby cries, the mother walks out of the room and leaves the baby alone.
   c. A mother shakes a rattle, the baby cries, the mother stops shaking the rattle.
   d. A baby cries, the mother picks up the baby, the baby stops crying; the next time the baby cries, the mother picks the baby up more quickly.

7. Social learning theory emphasizes the process of learning new behaviors by _____. (pp. 75-76)
   a. observing and imitating the behavior of others
   b. being taught by more skillful adults and peers
   c. being reinforced for increasingly close approximations of the desired behavior
   d. developing a cognitive map

8. Young children are scolded for being selfish; but when they are adults they are expected to be assertive and self-reliant. This is an example of _____. (p. 79)
   a. cultural conservatism
   b. cultural discontinuity
   c. worldview
   d. cultural continuity

9. Teacher and student, parent and child, salesperson and customer are all examples of _____. (p. 82)
   a. role strain
   b. role conflict
   c. childhood roles
   d. reciprocal roles

10. Among the seven theories presented, which one places the greatest emphasis on the interdependence among elements? (p. 83)
    a. social learning theory
    b. systems theory
    c. psychosexual theory
    d. evolutionary theory

After completing the post-test, compare your score with your performance on the pre-test. Can you identify areas where significant new learning has taken place? If you still have questions about some sections of the chapter, read them again. Check the glossary. You may want to discuss some of your questions with your instructor.

Step Eight: Suggestions for Further Observation and Study

1. Review the case of Robert Meyer and his adopted daughter, Juliet. Which of the theories presented in Chapter 3 help explain why Robert decided to become an adoptive parent? The various theories might offer different explanations.

2. Robert says that he spoils his child with all sorts of extras, and he works an additional job to afford this. What might be the consequences of this for Juliet? How do the learning theories, cognitive developmental theory, and social role theory account for this behavior?

3. Which of the seven theories presented in the chapter comes closest to your own personal theory of human behavior? Where did you learn these ideas? Which one is least familiar to you? Examine the ideas in that theory and relate them to what you already know.

4. Read biographical material about two of the theorists discussed in the chapter. What were some historical and intellectual forces that influenced the direction of their thinking? What life events may have channeled their interests toward the study of human behavior?

CHAPTER FOUR

The Period of Pregnancy and Prenatal Development

Step One: Review the Chapter Outline

Genetics and Development
    Genes and Chromosomes as Sources of Genetic Information
    The Laws of Heredity
        Alleles
        Genotype and Phenotype
        Sex-Linked Characteristics
    Genetic Sources of Individuality
        Genetic Determinants of Rate of Development
        Genetic Determinants of Individual Traits
        Genetic Determinants of Abnormal Development
    Genetic Technology and Psychosocial Evolution
        Mapping the Genome
        Ethical Considerations
    Evaluating the Impact of Heredity on Behavior
Normal Fetal Development
    Fertilization
        Twins
        Infertility and Alternative Means of Reproduction
    Development in the First Trimester
        The Germinal Period
        The Embryonic Period
        The Fetal Period
    Development in the Second Trimester
    Development in the Third Trimester
The Birth Process
    Stages of Labor
    Cesarean Delivery
    Infant Mortality
The Mother, the Fetus, and the Psychosocial Environment
    The Impact of the Fetus on the Pregnant Woman
        Changes in Roles and Social Status
        Changes in the Mother's Emotional State
        Fathers' Involvement during Pregnancy and Childbirth
    The Impact of the Pregnant Woman on the Fetus
        The Impact of Poverty
        Mother's Age
        Maternal Drug Use

      AIDS
      Environmental Toxins
      Obstetric Anesthetics
      Mother's Diet
   The Impact of Culture
      Reactions to Pregnancy
      Reactions to Childbirth
Applied Topic: Abortion
   The Legal Context of Abortion in the United States
   The Incidence of Legal Abortions
   The Impact of Abortion on Women
Chapter Summary
End of Chapter Case

Step Two: Review the Chapter Objectives

4.1   To describe the biochemical basis of genetic information and the process through which genetic information is transmitted from one generation to the next.

4.2   To identify the contributions of genetic factors to individuality through their role in controlling the rate of development, their contributions to individual traits, and the genetic sources of abnormalities.

4.3   To trace fetal development through three trimesters of pregnancy, including an understanding of critical periods of sensitivity to agent that may interfere with normal fetal development.

4.4   To describe the birth process and factors that contribute to infant mortality.

4.5   To analyze the reciprocity between the pregnant woman and the developing fetus, focusing on ways that pregnancy effects a childbearing woman and expectant father as well as basic influences on fetal growth such as maternal age, drug use, nutrition, and environmental toxins.

4.6   To examine the impact of culture on pregnancy and childbirth.

4.7   To analyze abortion from a psychosocial perspective including the legal context of abortion, the social and emotional impact of abortion for women, and men's views about abortion.

Step Three: Take the Pre-Test

Answer these questions before you read the chapter. The pages where material is discussed are indicated in the parentheses after each question. Use your performance as a guide to areas where you need to read especially carefully. The Answer Key for the pre-test can be found at the end of the study guide.

1. What is the biochemical basis of chromosomes? (p. 93)
   a. teratogens
   b. genes
   c. gametes
   d. DNA molecules

2. The alternate states of a gene on the two chromosome pairs are called _____. (p. 94)
   a. gametes
   b. genotypes
   c. alleles
   d. homozygous

3. What does it mean to say that hemophilia is a sex-linked trait? (p. 96)
   a. The gene for the trait is carried on the 23rd pair of chromosomes.
   b. The disease can only be observed in men.
   c. The disease is associated with abnormal sexual behavior.
   d. The gene for the trait is recessive.

4. The more similar two people are genetically, the more similar they will be with respect to _____. (pp. 96-102)
   a. height
   b. intelligence
   c. temperament
   d. all of these are correct.

5. During which period of fetal growth is the fetus *first* sensitive to touch, taste, and light? (p. 111)
   a. first trimester
   b. second trimester
   c. third trimester
   d. shortly after birth

6. Which organ of the developing fetus is vulnerable to the negative effects of teratogens for the longest period of time? (p. 109)
   a. the heart
   b. the eyes
   c. the arms and legs
   d. the central nervous system

Chapter 4

7. Which of the following is an example of how the developing fetus influences the pregnant woman? (pp. 118-119)
   a. Being pregnant changes a woman's social status.
   b. Pregnant women who smoke cigarettes have babies with low birth weight.
   c. Being pregnant usually has a calming, reassuring effect on a woman's emotional state.
   d. Women who are anxious about their pregnancy are likely to request more obstetrical anesthetics during labor.

8. How does the father's presence during labor and delivery usually effect childbirth? (p. 120)
   a. Babies are more alert at birth when fathers are present.
   b. Women are more irritable when the baby's father is present.
   c. Labor and delivery take longer when the father is present.
   d. Women have shorter labor when the baby's father is present.

9. Which of the following symptoms is associated with fetal alcohol syndrome? (p. 123)
   a. abnormalities of the legs and arms
   b. disorders of the central nervous system
   c. irritability and a high pitched cry.
   d. speech disorders

10. The beliefs, values, and practices associated with pregnancy and childbirth are known as the _____. (p. 126)
    a. infant mortality rate
    b. birth rate
    c. birth culture
    d. reaction range

Step Four: Read Chapter 4: The Period of Pregnancy and Prenatal Development

Step Five: Review Basic Concepts by Matching Each Term and Its Definition

a.	abortion	b.	allele
c.	artificial insemination	d.	chromosome
e.	genotype	f.	phenotype
g.	infant mortality rate	h.	gestational age
i	teratogen	j.	sex-linked trait
k.	reaction range	l.	solicitude

1. ( ) Infant deaths per 1000 live births.

2. ( ) Fertilization by medical injection of sperm.

3. ( ) Genetic characteristics, the genes for which are carried on the 23rd pair of chromosomes.

4. ( ) Termination of pregnancy before the fetus is able to survive outside the uterus.

5. ( ) The length of time since conception.

6. ( ) The hereditary information contained in the cells.

7. ( ) One of the long, thin strands of DNA found in the cell nucleus that carries genetic information.

8. ( ) Any agent that can produce a malformation in the developing fetus.

9. ( ) An attitude of care, interest, and helpfulness toward a pregnant woman.

10. ( ) Observable characteristics that result from the expression of a particular genotype in a specific environment.

11. ( ) Alternative states of a gene on the two paired chromosomes.

12. ( ) The variety of possible expressions of genetic information depending on the environmental conditions.

Step Six: Answer the Focusing Questions

1. Explain how genetic information is passed from the parent generation to the offspring. (pp. 93-95)

2. Describe the three ways that genetic information contributes to individual differences. (pp. 96-99)

3. How does the concept of a reaction range help explain how genetics and environment interact to produce observed behavior? (pp. 100-102)

4. Describe three or four major developmental milestones in each of the three trimesters of the prenatal period. At which period is the fetus most vulnerable to the disruptive effects of teratogens? (pp. 106-113)

5. The mother and the fetus are described as interdependent systems. Give three examples of ways that the fetus influences the mother, and three examples of ways the mother influences the fetus. (pp. 117-126)

6. What are some examples of solicitude vs shame and adequacy vs. vulnerability as they apply to how cultures view pregnancy and the pregnant couple? (pp. 126-129)

7. What appears to be the psychosocial impact of abortion for women and men? What new questions were raised in your mind as you read this section? (pp. 130-134)

_____

_____

_____

_____

Step Seven: Take the Post-Test

1. The portion of DNA that codes for one hereditary characteristic is called a _____. (p. 93)
   a. bond
   b. gene
   c. chromosome
   d. teratogen

2. The genetic information about a trait is the _____; the observed trait is the _____. (p. 94)
   a. dominance; co-dominance
   b. allele; chromosome
   c. genotype; phenotype
   d. phenotype; genotype

3. How is the mapping of the human genome related to genetic counseling? (pp. 99-100)
   a. Once the location of a genetic disease is identified, couples can be tested to see if either partner carries the gene.
   b. It allows people with a certain genetic disease to be paired with a partner who does not have the disease.
   c. It helps explain why genetic diseases are more likely in certain ethnic subgroups than in others.
   d. It gives the counselor more authority to decide if a couple should have a child or not.

4. When thinking about observed characteristics such as intelligence, temperament, or sociability, genetics is thought to establish the upper and lower limits of the trait, while the environment determines where along this continuum the behavior is actually observed. This concept is referred to as the _____. (pp. 100-101)
   a. phenotype
   b. sensitive period
   c. reaction range
   d. viability factor

Chapter 4

5. Which of the following is NOT an alternative means of reproduction used in cases of infertility? (p. 105)
   a. artificial insemination
   b. gamete intrafallopian transfer
   c. in vivo fertilization
   d. amniocentesis

6. Which of the following describes the embryo during the third and fourth weeks of gestation? (pp. 107-108)
   a. undergoing rapid cell differentiation
   b. responsive to taste and touch
   c. covered with soft, downy hair
   d. almost four inches long

7. Which of the following statements about infant mortality in the U.S. is true? (p. 117)
   a. The U.S. has the lowest infant mortality rate of the 20 leading industrialized countries in the world.
   b. Within the U. S. the region with the lowest infant mortality rate is Washington, D.C., because it is the nation's capitol and has access to more resources than other communities.
   c. Poverty is associated with high infant mortality rates.
   d. Infant mortality rates in the U.S. are the same for black and white babies.

8. How is a woman's age related to childbirth outcomes? (pp. 121-122)
   a. There is no systematic relationship between a woman's age and childbirth outcomes.
   b. Women between the ages of 16 and 35 have fewer complications in childbirth than younger or older women.
   c. Older women, that is over age 35, have shorter labors and fewer premature babies than do younger mothers.
   d. Younger mothers, that is under age 16, have healthier babies than do older mothers.

9. On a crowded subway, a young man gets up and gives his seat to a pregnant woman. This is an example of _____. (pp.127-128)
   a. solicitude
   b. shame
   c. couvade
   d. adequacy

10. Which of the following characteristics is associated with the most positive reactions to abortion? (pp. 133)
    a. a traditional gender-role orientation
    b. a view that abortion is acceptable, and that one's friends also see it as acceptable
    c. a late-term abortion
    d. being divorced or separated at the time of the abortion

Chapter 4

After completing the post-test, compare your score with your performance on the pre-test. Can you identify areas where significant new learning has taken place? If you still have questions about some sections of the chapter, read them again. Check the glossary. You may want to discuss some of your questions with your instructor.

Step Eight: Suggestions for Further Observation and Study

1. Review the case of Karen and Don. How did the realization that Don carried a genetic disease effect their family? What are the technical and ethical issues raised in this case?

2. Search the Internet for up-to-date information on alternative means of reproduction and the personal, health, and financial factors associated with a decision to try these methods.

3. Select a genetic anomaly, such as Tay Sachs disease, Sickle cell anemia, or some other condition that is especially likely in your own ethnic subgroup. Find out more information about diagnosis, treatment, and future prevention of that disease.

4. Visit a planned parenthood center in your community. Speak to the director or program coordinator about the types of services and programs provided by the center. What problems does the center face in serving its target population? How does the center evaluate its contribution to healthy pregnancies and low infant mortality rates in your community?

CHAPTER FIVE

Infancy (First 24 Months)

Step One: Review the Chapter Outline

Newborns
Developmental Tasks
    The Development of Sensory/Perceptual and Motor Functions
        Sensory/Perceptual Development
        Motor Development
        Temperament
    Attachment
        The Development of Attachment
        Formation of Attachments with Mother, Father, and Others
        Patterns of Attachment
        Parental Sensitivity and the Quality of Attachment
        The Relevance of Attachment to Later Development
    Sensorimotor Intelligence and Early Causal Schemes
        How do Infants Organize their Experiences?
        The Development of Causal Schemes
    Understanding The Nature of Objects and Creating Categories
        The Nature of Objects
        The Categorization of Objects
    Emotional Development
        Emotional Differentiation
        Emotions as a Key to Understanding Meaning
        The Ability to Regulate Emotions
        Emotions as a Channel for Adult-Infant Communication
The Psychosocial Crisis: Trust versus Mistrust
    Trust
    Mistrust
The Central Process for Resolving the Crisis: Mutuality with the Caregiver
        Coordination, Mismatch, and Repair of Interactions
        Establishing a Functional Rhythm in the Family
        Parents with Psychological Problems
The Prime Adaptive Ego Quality and the Core Pathology
    Hope
    Withdrawal

Applied Topic: The Role of Parents
    Safety in the Physical Environment
    Fostering Emotional and Cognitive Development
    Fathers' and Mothers' Parental Behavior
    Parents as Advocates
Chapter Summary
End of Chapter Case

Step Two: Review the Chapter Objectives

5.1   To identify important milestones in the maturation of the sensory and motor systems, and to describe the interactions among these systems during the first two years of life.

5.2   To define social attachment as the process through which infants develop strong emotional bonds with others, and to describe the dynamics of attachment formation during infancy.

5.3   To describe the development of sensorimotor intelligence, including an analysis of how infants organize experiences and conceptualize causality.

5.4   To examine how infants understand the properties of objects, including the sense that objects are permanent, that they have unique properties and functions, and that they can be categorized.

5.5   To examine the nature of emotional development, including emotional differentiation, the interpretation of emotions, and emotional regulation.

5.6   To analyze the factors that contribute to the resolution of the psychosocial crisis of trust versus mistrust, including the achievement of mutuality with the caregiver and the attainment of a sense of hope or withdrawal.

5.7   To evaluate the critical role of parents/caregivers during infancy with special attention to issues of safety in the physical environment; optimizing cognitive, social, and emotional development; and the role of parents/caregivers as advocates for their infants with other agencies and systems.

Step Three: Take the Pre-Test

Answer these questions before you read the text. The pages where the material is discussed are indicated in the parentheses after each question. Use your performance as a guide to areas where you need to read especially carefully. The Answer Key for the pre-test can be found at the end of the study guide.

1. Which of the following is used as evidence that an attachment has been formed? (p. 151)
   a. An infant calls to his or her attachment figure by name.
   b. An infant shows distress when the loved person comes near.
   c. An infant tries to maintain physical contact with the object of attachment.
   d. An infant acts more fussy in the afternoons than in the evenings.

2. Corey actively explores the living room at his aunt's house while his mother is sitting on the couch. When she leaves to get a drink in the kitchen, Corey fusses, but he calms down quickly as soon as she returns. Corey may be best described as having a(n) _____ attachment. (p. 154)
   a. anxious-avoidant
   b. secure
   c. anxious-resistant
   d. disorganized

3. Sensory experiences can strengthen certain neural pathways in the infant brain while less used pathways may disappear. This is called _____. (p. 141)
   a. flexibility
   b. plasticity
   c. neural responsivity
   d. visual acuity

4. Which of the following motor skills is not acquired during the first year of life? (p. 147)
   a. rolling over
   b. crawling
   c. standing alone
   d. running

5. Which of the following is an example of sensorimotor intelligence?
   a. sucking differently from a bottle and from a breast
   b. solving an arithmetic problem
   c. pretending to be a fireman
   d. using words as labels for objects

6. Ricky, who is 6 months old, discovers that if he lets his spoon drop it will fall to the floor and make a noise. He repeatedly drops his spoon and expresses great delight. This behavior is an example of _____. (p. 158)
   a. object permanence
   b. imprinting
   c. sensorimotor causality
   d. attachment

7. A six-month-old baby is playing with a rattle. It drops from her hand, and she does not look around for it. This suggests that she has not developed _____. (p. 160)
   a. object permanence
   b. a scheme
   c. categorization skills
   d. circular reactions

8. Which of the following is among the earliest emotions to be expressed in infancy, before 6 months of age? (p. 164)
   a. pleasure
   b. pride
   c. defiance
   d. guilt

9. In infancy, trust refers to the infant's sense that he or she is _____. (p. 169)
   a. intelligent
   b. creative
   c. skillful and resourceful
   d. valued

10. Which of the following is the central process for resolving the psychosocial crisis of infancy? (p. 172)
    a. education
    b. mutuality with the caregiver
    c. imitation
    d. social support

Step Four: Read Chapter 5: Infancy

Step Five: Review Basic Concepts By Matching Each Term and Its Definition

a.	critical period	b.	mistrust
c.	mutuality	d.	object permanence
e.	sensorimotor intelligence	f.	separation anxiety
g.	social attachment	h.	synchrony
i.	temperament	j.	trust
k.	emotional regulation	l.	intersubjectivity

1. ( ) Strategies for dealing with intense emotions.

2. ( ) Rhythmic, well-timed, appropriately responsive interactions.

3. ( ) A time of maximum sensitivity to or readiness for the development of a particular skill or behavior pattern.

4. ( ) A strong, affectionate bond that develops between infants and their caregivers.

5. ( ) The ability of two people to meet each other's needs and share each other's concerns and feelings.

6. ( ) Feelings of fear or sadness associated with the departure of the attachment figure.

7. ( ) An emotional sense that the environment is capable of meeting one's basic needs and that one is worthy of the love of others.

8. ( ) Relatively stable characteristics of response to environmental stimuli, largely under genetic control.

9. ( ) The ability of two or more people to know what one another is experiencing.

10. ( ) A sense of unpredictability in the environment and suspicion about one's own worth. Doubt that one's needs will be met.

11. ( ) A scheme acquired during the sensorimotor stage of development in which infants become aware that an object continues to exist even when it is hidden or moved from place to place.

12. ( ) In Piaget's theory of development, the first stage of cognitive growth during which schema are established on the basis of sensory and motor experiences.

Step Six: Answer the Focusing Questions

1. What are the five common stages in the development of social attachment? What behaviors are characteristic of each stage? (p. 151)

_____

_____

_____

_____

2. Describe the four patterns of attachment noting the behaviors that are characteristic of the infant and the parenting behaviors that are likely to lead to the development of each pattern. (pp. 153-154)

3. List the major competencies in each of the following domains of the sensory/perceptual system that occur during the first few months of life. (pp. 141-145)

4. Define sensorimotor intelligence and briefly describe each of the six phases in the development of causal schemes. (pp. 157-160, Table p. 159)

5. What is object permanence, how is it studied, and why is it important? (pp. 160-163)

6. Identify the major events that occur in the differentiation, interpretation, and regulation of emotion during infancy. (pp. 164-168)

7. In what ways is an infant prepared from birth or shortly thereafter to participate in social interactions? (pp. 168-169)

8. Describe the processes through which infants and caregivers achieve mutuality in their interactions. (pp. 172-174)

9. In your own words, describe the most important things parents can do to foster optimal development in their infants. (pp. 176-179)

Chapter 5

Step Seven: Take the Post-Test

1. During the second half of the first year, two signs of a child's growing attachment to a specific other person are observed. (pp. 151-153)
    a. first habits and circular reactions.
    b. rooting and grasping.
    c. intersubjectivity and matching.
    d. stranger anxiety and separation anxiety.

2. A critical period refers to which of the following? (p. 170)
    a. a time of maximal readiness for the development of some behavior
    b. a time in life when a person has to make an important life decision
    c. a time of intense interaction between parents and babies
    d. a life stage that is more important than other life stages

3. Which of the following sensory/motor systems is least well developed in newborns? (p. 145)
    a. vision
    b. hearing
    c. taste
    d. voluntary motor activity

4. Which of the following statements about temperament is the most accurate? (p. 149)
    a. Infant reflexes are a result of a child's temperament.
    b. Activity level, sociability, and emotionality are relatively stable components of a child's temperament.
    c. Temperament refers to components of a child's personality that are out of control.
    d. For the most part, temperament is a product of socialization experiences.

5. According to Piaget's theory, what is the primary mechanism underlying the growth of intelligence during infancy? (p. 157)
    a. sensorimotor adaptation
    b. synchrony
    c. assimilation
    d. intersubjectivity

6. The first phase in the development of causal schemes is the phase of _____. (p. 159)
    a. insight
    b. circular reactions
    c. smiling
    d. reflexes

7. The domain of emotions is a two-way channel through which infants and their caregivers can establish _____. (p. 168)
   a. social referencing
   b. cognitive maturation
   c. intersubjectivity
   d. psychosocial crisis

8. Mistrust may develop if a caregiver is unusually harsh while meeting an infant's needs or if _____. (p. 170)
   a. the caregiver caters to the child's every whim.
   b. the caregiver cannot identify the child's needs and respond appropriately to them.
   c. the caregiver responds too quickly.
   d. the caregiver talks to the infant too much.

9. Within the process of communication, the pattern of coordination, mismatch, and repair builds a sense of _____ between the infant and the caregiver. (p. 172)
   a. mistrust
   b. anxiety
   c. causality
   d. mutuality

10. In their parental roles, mothers in the United States tend to emphasize _____ while fathers tend to emphasize _____. (p. 178)
    a. physical play; caregiving
    b. the process of development; product
    c. object permanence; the development of causal schemes
    d. intersubjectivity; communication repair

After completing the post-test, compare your score with your performance on the pre-test. Can you identify areas where significant new learning has taken place? If you still have questions about some sections of the chapter, read them again. Check the glossary. You may want to discuss some of your questions with your instructor.

Step Eight: Suggestions for Further Observation and Study

1. Visit the newborn nursery of a hospital and watch the babies for half an hour. Keep an observation log of what you observe. Can you detect individual differences in responsiveness, activity level, or irritability? Do you notice babies starting to cry in response to the crying of other babies?

2. Construct a chart that draws together all the factors discussed in the chapter that influence an infant's capacity to engage in social interaction.

3. Review recent literature on the impact of day care or alternative child care arrangements on development during infancy. Develop a list of recommendations about infant child care that parents could use when considering whether to place an infant in child care and what the best kind of arrangement would be.

4. Ask some adults, adolescents, and young children what trust and mistrust mean to them. Ask them to describe to you how they know when they can trust someone or when the cannot. How does the use of these terms differ for the three different age levels? How do the popular uses of these words compare to the psychosocial meanings discussed in the text?

5. Imagine that you are responsible for the care of an infant where you currently live. What are the potential risks and hazards of your home environment for the infant? What steps would you take to reduce risks and increase the baby's safety in your home? As you think about this, do you prefer the strategy of restricting the baby to keep her or him safe, or the strategy of altering the environment to permit maximum exploration?

CHAPTER SIX

Toddlerhood (Ages 2 and 3)

Step One: Review the Chapter Outline

Developmental Tasks
    Elaboration of Locomotion
    Fantasy Play
        Semiotic Thinking
        The Nature of Pretend Play
        The Capacity for Pretense
        Changes in Fantasy Play During Toddlerhood
        The Contribution of Fantasy Play to Development
        The Role of Play Companions
        Imaginary Companions
    Language Development
        Communication Accomplishments in Infancy
        Communicative Competence in Toddlerhood
        Language Development Beyond Toddlerhood
        The Language Environment
    Self-Control
        Control of Impulses
        Individual Differences in the Ability to Control Impulses
        Self-Regulated Goal Attainment
The Psychosocial Crisis: Autonomy versus Shame and Doubt
    Autonomy
    Shame and Doubt
The Central Process: Imitation
The Prime Adaptive Ego Quality and The Core Pathology
    Will
    Compulsion
The Impact of Poverty on Psychosocial Development in Toddlerhood
Applied Topic: Day Care
    The Impact of Day Care
        Intelligence and Academic Achievement
        Social Competence
        Peer Relations
    Directions for the Future
Chapter Summary
End of Chapter Case

Step Two: Review the Chapter Objectives

6.1 To describe the expansion of locomotor skills during toddlerhood, indicating their importance for the child's
expanding capacity to explore the environment and experience opportunities for mastery.

6.2 To examine the development of fantasy play and its importance for cognitive and social development.

6.3 To document accomplishments in language development and describe the major influence of interactive experiences and the language environment for the process of language acquisition.

6.4 To examine the development of self-control, especially impulse management and goal attainment, highlighting strategies young children use to help them regulate their actions.

6.5 To analyze the psychosocial crisis of autonomy versus shame and doubt, to clarify the central process of imitation, and to describe the prime adaptive ego strength of will and the core pathology of compulsion.

6.6 To apply a psychosocial analysis to the topic of day care, emphasizing the impact of the social environment on patterns of development during toddlerhood.

Step Three: Take the Pre-Test

Answer these questions before you read the text. The pages where the material is discussed are indicated in the parentheses after each question. Use your performance as a guide to areas where you need to read especially carefully. The Answer Key for the pre-test can be found at the end of the study guide.

1. The primary motivation for the abundant activity of toddlers is _____. (p. 184)
    a. nurturance
    b. approval
    c. mastery
    d. affiliation

2. The basis for which two fundamental movement patterns seem to be developed during toddlerhood. (p. 186)
    a. running and jumping
    b. skipping rope
    c. climbing
    d. rolling over

3. Which of the following is an example of symbolic play? (p. 188)
    a. playing the drums
    b. playing house
    c. playing with one's toes
    d. playing with a rattle

4. What is the meaning of the term holophase? (p. 195)
   a. vocalization without meaning
   b. two-word sentences
   c. grammatical transformations
   d. single word utterances accompanied by gestures, action, vocal intonation, and emotion

5. Which of the following terms refers to an adult strategy for enhancing children's language development by asking a question that urges the child to say more? (p. 203)
   a. prompting
   b. motherese
   c. expansion
   d. semantic contingency

6. Which of the following is NOT a strategy that toddlers use to achieve self-control? (p. 207)
   a. talking to themselves
   b. diverting their attention to something else
   c. insisting on having their own way
   d. creating an imaginary situation in which disturbing problems can be expressed and resolved

7. Which of the following is an example of autonomy? (p. 211)
   a. Nobody likes me.
   b. That's not fair.
   c. I can do it myself.
   d. I hate you.

8. Which of the following is a example of imitation? (p. 213)
   a. repeating a story told by father
   b. believing in the tooth fairy
   c. making up a story
   d. banging pots together

9. Which of the following is a form of discipline in which the caregiver points out the consequences of a certain behavior and redirects the child's behavior? (p. 206)
   a. induction
   b. love withdrawal
   c. power assertion
   d. time out

10. Which of the following has been documented as a positive consequence of participation in quality day care? (p. 218)
   a. improved memorization skills
   b. higher levels of social competence, self-esteem, and empathy
   c. higher IQ scores in adolescence and adulthood
   d. better chances of receiving a college scholarship

Step Four: Read Chapter 6: Toddlerhood (Ages 2 and 3)

Step Five: Review Basic Concepts By Matching Each Term and Its Definition

a.	autonomy	b.	communicative competence
c.	discipline	d.	imitation
e.	induction	f.	love withdrawal
g.	power assertion	h.	preoperational thought
i.	self-control	j.	shame
k.	scaffolding	l.	symbolic play

1. ( ) The ability to use all aspects of language in order to produce and interpret communication.

2. ( ) Explanations that point out the consequences of a behavior for others.

3. ( ) In Piaget's theory of cognitive development, the stage during which representational skills are acquired.

4. ( ) The ability to restrain impulses and the ability to function as a causal agent.

5. ( ) The ability to do things on one's own.

6. ( ) Strategies for punishing or changing behavior.

7. ( ) The creation of pretend characters, objects, and situations in play.

8. ( ) Repetitions of another person's words, gestures, or actions.

9. ( ) The process through which an adult and child arrive at a shared understanding and then the adult interacts so as to expand the child's communicative competence.

10. ( ) A discipline technique in which a parent's size and strength are used to dominate a child.

11. ( ) An emotional response to being discovered doing something wrong.

12. ( ) A discipline technique in which a child's behavior can result in loss of parental affection.

Step Six: Answer the Focusing Questions

1. What are some of the significant achievements in the toddler's capacity for locomotion? (pp. 185-187)

   _____

   _____

   _____

   _____

   _____

2. What are the five representational skills acquired during toddlerhood? (p. 188)

   _____

   _____

   _____

   _____

3. What are the four dimensions along which the capacity for fantasy play changes during toddlerhood? (p. 189)

   _____

   _____

   _____

   _____

   _____

4. In what ways do caregivers contribute to language acquisition during toddlerhood? (pp. 200-204)

5. How do language and symbolic play differ as strategies the toddler can use for expressing inner feelings and for solving problems? (p. 207)

6. What are the factors that contribute to a toddler's growing ability to exercise self-control? What factors interfere with this ability? (pp. 204-209)

7. How might different discipline techniques contribute to the resolution of the psychosocial crisis of autonomy versus shame and doubt? (pp. 206, 211-213)

8. What is the controversy regarding day care in the United States? What are the psychosocial needs of toddlers that must be considered as this controversy is resolved? (pp. 217-221)

_____

_____

_____

_____

Step Seven: Take the Post-Test

1. The use of the term toddler highlights which aspect of development during toddlerhood? (p. 185)
   a. mental representation
   b. locomotion
   c. discipline
   d. language development

2. Which of the following is an example of preoperational thought? (p. 187)
   a. crying
   b. playing cards
   c. throwing a ball
   d. pretending to be a superhero

3. Which of the following characteristics is associated with well-developed fantasy play skills? (pp. 189-190)
   a. social isolation
   b. flexible problem solving skills
   c. poor verbal communication skills
   d. daydreaming and inability to focus

4. _____ and _____ appear to travel independent courses that intersect during the second year of life. (p. 194)
   a. action; thought
   b. action; reaction
   c. thought; language
   d. reality; fantasy

5. A major accomplishment in language development during the second year of life is the child's ability to _____. (p. 196)
   a. vocalize
   b. babble
   c. use the grammatically correct form of singular, possessive pronouns
   d. form two-word sentences

6. How does a parent's use of expansion help a child develop communication skills? (p. 202)
   a. It elaborates on the child's expression.
   b. It avoids forcing the child to speak.
   c. It moves to a level of greater abstraction.
   d. It urges the child to listen more carefully.

7. One of the important elements of self-control that develops during toddlerhood is the ability to _____. (p. 204)
   a. delay the gratification or expression of impulses
   b. express impulses quickly
   c. regress to an earlier form of impulse gratification
   d. feel out of control

8. The primary motivation for imitation in toddlerhood is the drive for _____. (p. 213)
   a. affiliation
   b. mastery and competence
   c. power
   d. generativity

9. Which of the following statements about discipline is true? (p. 206)
   a. Effective punishments should not have to repeated frequently.
   b. Parents who use inductions create high levels of anxiety in their children.
   c. The use of power assertion promotes the internalization of moral standards.
   d. Children must know which acts are considered appropriate in order to correct their behavior.

10. Which of the statements about the impact of day care is false? (pp. 217-221)
    a. Children who have had quality day care experiences tend to show higher levels of empathy.
    b. Children who have had quality day care experiences are less compliant with their parents.
    c. Children who have been in the same day care center for a long period of time develop more complex peer play skills.
    d. Children who have had quality day care experiences are more likely to play alone and to be described as shy.

After completing the post-test, compare your score with your performance on the pre-test. Can you identify areas where significant new learning has taken place? If you still have questions about some sections of the chapter, read them again. You may want to discuss some of your questions with your instructor.

Step Eight: Suggestions for Further Observation and Study

1. What can you recall about the nature of your own fantasy play when you were a toddler? Ask your parents or older siblings what they can remember. What kinds of pretense did you enjoy? What sorts of characters or situations did you create? Did you have some special props or toys that were central to your pretense? Who were your play companions and what kinds of group fantasy activities did you create?

2. As a 2 ½ or 3 year old to explain a game to you or to tell you how a toy works. What special qualities do you notice about this child's use of language?

3. Read the advice to parents about discipline that is provided in two or three parenting books available in your local bookstore. How does that advice compare to the research evidence on discipline techniques discussed in the text?

4. Visit a day care center. Watch the children at play. What kinds of experiences seem to contribute to autonomy in this setting? What factors might interfere with autonomy or produce feelings of shame and doubt?

CHAPTER SEVEN

Early School Age (4 to 6 years)

Step One: Review the Chapter Outline

Developmental Tasks
    Gender Identification
        Individual Differences versus Constructivism
        Understanding Gender
        Sex-Role Standards
        Identification with Parents
        Gender Preference
    Early Moral Development
        Learning Theory
        Cognitive-Development Theory
        Psychoanalytic Theory
        Research on Empathy and Perspective Taking
        Research on Parental Discipline
        The Impact of Television on Moral Development
        Review
    Self-Theory
        Developmental Changes in the Self-Theory
        Self-Esteem
    Group Play
        Group Games
        Friendship Groups
The Psychosocial Crisis: Initiative versus Guilt
    Initiative
    Guilt
The Central Process: Identification
The Prime Adaptive Ego Quality and the Core Pathology
    Purpose
    Ambition
Applied Topic: School Readiness
    Readiness
    How to Measure Kindergarten Readiness?
    What Obstacles Stand in the Way of School Readiness?
    Supporting Children with Disabilities
    Who is Responsible for Meeting the Goal for School Readiness?
Chapter Summary
End of Chapter Case

Step Two: Review the Chapter Objectives

7.1 To describe the process of gender identification during early school age and its importance for the way a child interprets his or her experiences.

7.2 To describe the process of early moral development, drawing from research and theories to explain how knowledge, emotion, and action combine to produce internalized morality

7.3 To analyze changes in the self-theory, with special focus on self-evaluation and self-esteem during the early school-age years.

7.4 To explore the transition to more complex group play and the process of friendship development in the early school-age years.

7.5 To explain the psychosocial crisis of initiative versus guilt, the central process of identification, the prime adaptive ego function of purpose, and the core pathology of inhibition.

7.6 To consider social expectations for school readiness, its relation to the developmental tasks of early school age, and the obstacles that may prevent children from being able to adept and learn in the school environment.

Step Three: Take the Pre-Test

Answer these questions before you read the text. The pages where the material is discussed are indicated in the parentheses after each question. Use your performance as a guide to areas where you need to read especially carefully. The Answer Key for the pre-test can be found at the end of this study guide.

1. Which is the earliest component of sex-role identification to be achieved? (p. 227)
    a. sex-role standards
    b. sex-role preference
    c. gender label
    d. sex-role identification

2. Which of the following has not been proposed as a motive for parental identification? (pp. 230-231)
    a. need for status
    b. fear of loss of love
    c. identification with the aggressor
    d. fear of failure

3. Which of the following theories views moral behavior as a result of repeated associations between valued behavior and reinforcements? (pp. 234-235)
    a. psychoanalytic theory
    b. learning theory
    c. cognitive-developmental theory
    d. social-role theory

4. According to cognitive-developmental theory, how do early school age children determine whether an action is right or wrong? (pp. 235-236)
   a. They focus on the consequences of the action.
   b. They depend on the evaluation of the action by peers.
   c. They look at the benefit of the action to society.
   d. They base their decision on the principle of human rights.

5. Which statement best reflects a 4 to 6 year old child's social perspective-taking ability? Early school age children _____. (pp. 239-240)
   a. assume that everyone involved views a situation just as they do
   b. realize that a situation may look very different to someone who is not involved in the situation as it appears to them
   c. are able to recognize that people may feel different emotions in the same situation
   d. realize that people can take each other's point of view into account before they decide to act.

6. The text treats the _____ as a theory that links a person's understanding about the nature of the world, the nature of the self, and the meaning of interactions between the self and the environment. (p. 244)
   a. reward structure
   b. self-concept
   c. superego
   d. sex-role preference

7. In the group games of early school age children, they learn about _____. (p. 249)
   a. out-group attitudes
   b. teams
   c. exchanging roles
   d. complex rule structures

8. Which of the following is the best definition for the psychosocial concept of initiative? (pp. 251-252)
   a. active investigation of the environment
   b. a sense of pride in a job well-done
   c. anxiety caused by having violated a cultural norm
   d. a caring orientation toward relationships

9. Normal levels of guilt are positively associated with _____. (p. 253)
   a. fear of school
   b. creative problem solving
   c. hostile feelings toward teachers
   d. remorse and attempts to set things right

10. Research indicates that one consequence for children of viewing televised violence is _____. (pp. 241-242)
    a. an increase in the child's dislike of violence
    b. an increase in the child's fear of his/her father
    c. an increase in the child's repertoire of aggressive behaviors
    d. a decrease in the child's need to be aggressive

Step Four: Read Chapter 7: Early School Age (4 to 6 years)

Step Five: Review Basic Concepts by Matching Each Term and Its Definition

a.	self-esteem	b.	self-theory
c.	sex-role standards	d.	sex-role preference
e.	empathy	f.	gender label
g.	group play	h.	guilt
i.	identification	j.	initiative
k.	perspective-taking	l.	preconventional morality

1. ( )   Active experimentation and investigation of the environment.

2. ( )   A theory that links a person's understanding of the nature of the world, the nature of the self, and the meaning of interactions between the self and the environment.

3. ( )   The capacity to recognize and experience the emotional state of another person.

4. ( )   The evaluative dimension of the self that includes feelings of worthiness, pride, and discouragement.

5. ( )   Cultural norms about the attributes that should characterize males and females.

6. ( )   A psychosocial mechanism in which people incorporate valued characteristics of important others.

7. ( )   A word that indicates the sex of a person.

8.   ( )   An early form of game such as "Ring Around the Rosie" that has a ritualized format and few rules.

9.   ( )   An emotion associated with doing something wrong or anticipating doing something wrong.

10. ( )   A positive value for being a member of one gender group or the other.

11. ( )   In Kohlberg's scheme, the first stage of moral development when judgments are based on the consequences of behavior.

12. ( )   The ability to take the point of view of another, especially when that person's point of view is different from one's own.

Step Six: Answer the Focusing Questions

1.   What is the difference between the individual differences perspective and the constructivist perspective for explaining gender differences? (p. 227)

_____

_____

_____

_____

2.   What are four dimensions of sex-role identification? Give an example of each. (p. 227)

_____

_____

_____

_____

_____

_____

3. How do Rewards and Punishments, Empathy, Perspective Taking, Moral Standards, Parental Discipline, Moral Reasoning and Parental Identification contribute to morality during the early school age period? (pp. 234-241)

4. What is self-theory? (pp. 244-249)

5. What is self-esteem? Why might the early school age group period be a time when self-esteem is especially vulnerable to fluctuations? (pp. 246-249)

6. How does identification contribute to the resolution of the psychosocial crisis of initiative versus guilt? (pp. 254-255)

7. Compare and contrast parents' and teachers' measures of kindergarten readiness. (p. 258)

8. Who is responsible for meeting the national goal for school readiness? (p. 259)

Step Seven: Take the Post-Test

1. Which of the following motives for parental identification is aroused by the following statement: "You and your father have the same sense of humor." (pp. 230-231)
    a. perceived similarity
    b. identification with the future
    c. fear of loss of love
    d. identification with the aggressor

2. If parents wish for a boy, but give birth to a girl, the child may have difficulty establishing _____. (p. 232)
    a. peer-group friendships
    b. sex-role preference
    c. sex-role standards
    d. morality

3. Cognitive developmental theorists and learning theorists agree that which of the following guides the very young child's moral judgments? (pp. 234-237)
    a. conscience
    b. rewards and punishments
    c. empathy
    d. a sense of justice

Chapter 7

4. A toddler offers her own favorite cuddly blanket to her father when he hurts his leg. This is an example of which type of empathy? (p. 238)
   a. empathy for another's feelings
   b. empathy for another's life conditions
   c. global empathy
   d. egocentric empathy

5. Albert is the only child in his entire second grade class whose parents have separated. When children talk about their homes, their parents, or their families, Albert has strong feelings of embarrassment and lack of worth. This is an example of _____. (p. 247)
   a. self-esteem
   b. preconventional morality
   c. contextual dissonance
   d. initiative

6. Which of the following statements about group play is true? (p. 249)
   a. Group games require a referee or umpire in order to be played fairly.
   b. Group games usually involve opposing teams.
   c. Group games usually involve a fantasy element.
   d. Group game require strict division of roles and responsibilities.

7. Which of the following statements about friendship during the early school age period is true? (p. 250)
   a. friendships are based on loyalty and trust
   b. children of this age rarely argue or quarrel during play
   c. boys and girls usually play together
   d. boys and girls tend to pick friends of the same sex

8. Which term refers to the psychological mechanism that signals when a violation of a forbidden behavior or thought is about to occur? (pp. 252-254)
   a. fixation
   b. mistrust
   c. guilt
   d. phobia

9. Which of the following is a consequence of watching television? (p. 242)
   a. It decreases participation in community and recreational activities.
   b. It helps children view the world as a safe, caring place.
   c. It increases social interaction.
   d. It decreases interest in commercial products such as toys, candy, and cereal.

10. Which of the following may be considered an example of how television could promote optimal development? (p.242)
    a. watching television might reduce a child's social interactions
    b. watching television might help children experience empathy for others
    c. watching television might lead to expectations that problems can be easily solved
    d. watching television might lower a child's self-esteem

After completing the post-test, compare your score with your performance on the pre-test. Can you identify where significant new learning has taken place? If you still have questions about sections of the chapter, read them again. You may want to discuss some of your questions with your instructor.

Step Eight: Suggestions for Further Observation and Study

1. Find out what you can about sex-role standards among African American, Asian American, and Latino subcultures. In what ways do the ethnic groups differ in their expectations about the behavior role of male and female children?

2. Ask three children ages 4, 6, and 8 what it means to cheat and whether there are some reasons that cheating may be permissible. Compare their answers. Look for evidence of their understanding of the rules, their level of moral judgment, and their ability to take another person's perspective.

3. Read Piaget's The Moral Judgment of the Child and the section of Freud's Introductory Lectures on Psychoanalysis that deals with the formation of the superego. How do these theorists differ in their analysis of the formation of morality during childhood? What are the similarities between the two?

4. Talk with some parents about how their children coped with the process of attending kindergarten. How did this school transition affect the four developmental tasks for each child? What changes occurred in the groups influencing the child and in their relative importance in the child's life?

5. Watch an hour or two of children's television. What assumptions do television producers appear to make about the kinds of entertainment that are suitable for children?

Chapter 7

CHAPTER EIGHT

Middle Childhood (6-12 Years)

Step One: Review the Chapter Outline

Developmental Tasks
    Friendship
        Family Influences on Social Competence
        Three Contributions of Friendship to Social Development
        Loneliness
        Close Friends
    Concrete Operations
        Conservation
        Classification Skills
        Combinatorial Skills
        Metacognition
    Skill Learning
        Features of Skilled Learning
        Reading
        A Model of the Developing Mind
        The Social Context of Skill Development
    Self-Evaluation
        Self-Efficacy
        Social Expectations
    Team Play
        Interdependence
        Division of Labor
        Competition
        In-Group and Out-Group Attitudes
The Psychosocial Crisis: Industry versus Inferiority
    Industry
    Inferiority
The Prime Adaptive Ego Quality and the Core Pathology
    Competence
    Inertia
Applied Topic: Violence in the Lives of Children
    Consequences of Exposure to Violence
    Prevention Strategies
Chapter Summary
End of Chapter Case

Step Two: Review the Chapter Objectives

8.1 To clarify the role of friendship in helping children to learn to take the point of view of others, be sensitive to the norms and pressures of the peer group, and experience closeness in relationships as well as to clarify negative consequences that result from social rejection and loneliness.

8.2 To describe the development of concrete operational thought, including conservation, classification skills, combinatorial skills, and the child's ability to understand and monitor his or her own knowledge and understanding.

8.3 To explore skill learning, including the presentation of a model for the process of acquisition of complex skills such as reading and the examination of societal factors that provide the context within which skill learning occurs.

8.4 To analyze the development of self-evaluation skills, including self-efficacy, and ways that social expectations of parents, teachers, and peers contribute to a child's self-evaluation.

8.5 To describe a new level of complexity in play as children become involved in team sports and athletic competition.

8.6 To explain the psychosocial crisis of industry versus inferiority, the central process through which the crisis is resolved – education- the prime adaptive ego quality of competence, and the core pathology of inertia.

8.7 To explore the impact of exposure to violence on development during middle childhood.

Step Three: Take the Pre-Test

Answer these questions before you read the text. The pages where the material is discussed are indicated in the parentheses after each question. Use your performance as a guide to areas where you need to read especially carefully. The Answer Key for the pre-test can be found at the end of the study guide.

1. Theories about development during middle childhood age tend to emphasize _____. (p. 264)
    a. sexuality
    b. intellectual growth
    c. emotional changes
    d. parent-child conflict

2. Peer interaction helps reduce _____. (p. 266)
    a. egocentrism
    b. flexibility
    c. assimilation
    d. conservation

3. Which of the following is the best definition of conservation? (p. 271)
   a. what has been done can be undone
   b. objects can be grouped together in categories
   c. categories have a hierarchical relationship to one another
   d. physical matter does not appear or disappear despite changes in form or container

4. Classification skills require which ability? (pp. 273-274)
   a. ordering subgroups in a hierarchy
   b. manipulating numbers
   c. taking another person's point of view
   d. conserving volume

5. Which of the following statements about reading achievement is most accurate? (p. 277)
   a. Reading is a trial and error process that does not involve the use of strategies.
   b. All children learn to read in the same manner.
   c. One of the most important activities that promotes reading achievement is reading.
   d. Parents have little influence on their child's reading achievement.

6. Children who doubt that they have the ability to succeed in a task are more likely to_____. (p. 283)
   a. seek more difficult challenges
   b. try harder
   c. give up
   d. learn new skills

7. How do social expectations influence a child's self-evaluation? (p. 284)
   a. social expectations influence a child's confidence about success or failure
   b. social expectations influence a child's categorization skills
   c. social expectations create areas of talent
   d. social expectations foster out-group attitudes

8. Participation in team play helps children learn _____. (pp. 287-288)
   a. conservation of volume
   b. the relationship of subgroups to hierarchies
   c. the importance of division of labor in activities
   d. the meaning of egocentrism

9. Psychosocial theory states one's basic attitudes toward _____ is formed during the middle childhood period. (p. 291)
   a. authority figures
   b. work
   c. children
   d. love

10. Cultures devise ways of passing on the wisdom and skills of past generations to its children through _____. (p. 294)
    a. laws
    b. rules
    c. reading
    d. education

Step Four: Read Chapter 8: Middle Childhood (6-12 Years)

Step Five: Review Basic Concepts by Matching Each Term and Its Definition

a.	peers	b.	classification
c.	social expectations	d.	industry
e.	inferiority	f.	self-efficacy
g.	conservation	h.	concrete operational thought
i.	metacognition	j.	hypercognitive system
k.	education	l.	division of labor

1. ( ) A sense of pride and pleasure in acquiring culturally valued competencies.

2. ( ) All the functions that allow one to assess the meaning of a task and evaluate what will be required to perform it.

3. ( ) Views held by others about what would be appropriate behavior in a given situation or stage of development.

4. ( ) Persons belonging to the same group, often on the basis of age or grade.

5. ( ) A sense of confidence that one can perform the behaviors required in a given situation.

6. ( ) Grouping objects according to some characteristics they have in common, including all objects that show the characteristic and none that do not.

7. ( ) Thinking about and monitoring one's own thinking.

8. ( ) A sense of incompetence and failure which is built on negative evaluations and lack of skill.

9. ( ) The principle that complex tasks can best be performed when individuals assume special functions and coordinate their efforts.

10. ( )   The concept that changes in shape or container do not alter the mass, weight, number, or volume of matter.

11. ( )   The process of passing on the wisdom and skills of past generations to the young.

12. ( )   In Piaget's theory, a stage of cognitive development in which rules of logic are applied to observable, physical relationships.

Step Six: Answer the Focusing Questions

1. How do friendships and peer interactions promote cognitive and social development during the middle childhood age period?   (pp. 265-270)

2. How might the cognitive capacities for conservation, classification, and combinatorial processes influence the middle childhood age child's social relationships and self-evaluation?   (pp. 271-274)

3. Review Figure 8.2 on page 279. How do each of the three structural systems – the processing system, the hypercognitive system, and the specialized structural system – contribute to addressing a complex intellectual task, such as studying for an hour exam in your human development course?

4. In what ways might teachers' expectations influence a child's sense of industry or inferiority? (pp. 284-285)

5. How might experiences in team play contribute to a child's cognitive development? (pp. 287-291)

6. How can parents and teachers work together to promote a sense of industry and academic excellence in middle childhood age children? (pp. 294-296)

Step Seven: Take the Post-Test

1. In which theory is the middle childhood age period referred to as latency? (p. 264)
   a. psychosocial theory
   b. psychoanalytic theory
   c. social learning theory
   d. cognitive developmental theory

Chapter 8

2. Peer relations differ from parent-child relations in which of the following ways? (pp. 265-270)
   a. peers never have conflicts about power, but parents and children do
   b. peers have more power over one another than parents have over their children
   c. peers are more equal in power than parents and children
   d. peers have more resources than parents

3. Which three concepts are central to the capacity to conserve? (pp. 271-272)
   a. volume, space, relativity
   b. operation, classification, reciprocity
   c. identity, reversibility, reciprocity
   d. classification, reversibility, ordering

4. Which of the following statements best describes how complex skill are learned? (pp. 278-280)
   a. Skilled behavior relies on routine memorization rather than on cognitive strategies.
   b. Complex skills are attained through an integration of many levels of the component elements at once.
   c. Complex skills are learned in a strict sequence.
   d. Complex skills require separating the sensory and the motor components.

5. Which of the following is a source of information upon which judgments of self-efficacy are based? (p. 283)
   a. reversibility
   b. fantasies
   c. enactive attainments
   d. grade in school

6. Which of the following is likely to occur if a teacher has low expectations for a child's performance? (p. 285)
   a. The child will perform less well than if the teacher had higher expectations.
   b. The child's performance will not be related to the teacher's expectations
   c. The child will do better to prove the teacher wrong
   d. The teacher will feel frustrated by the child's failure.

7. Which of the following is an "out-group" attitude? (p. 290)
   a. to take personal satisfaction in team successes
   b. to relinquish personal goals for team goals
   c. to work one's hardest to defeat the other team
   d. to value and use feedback from team members

8. What is the psychosocial crisis of the middle childhood age period?
   a. initiative versus guilt
   b. trust versus mistrust
   c. autonomy versus shame and doubt
   d. industry versus inferiority

9. What does the term "contextualizing instruction" mean? (p. 295)
   a. Grading the brightest children and teaching the lower ability children on a pass-fail basis.
   b. Creating a system of contracts in each subject.
   c. Insisting all children adapt to the same school culture.
   d. Creating a classroom environment that recognizes and builds upon children's prior experiences. and previous knowledge.

10. A public health perspective on strategies to prevent violence focuses on _____. (p. 300)
    a. controlling aggressive children
    b. a collaboration in identifying various layers of prevention
    c. the criminal justice definitions and strategies for deterrence
    d. first controlling the television programs geared toward children

After completing the post-test, compare your score with your performance on the pre-test. Can you identify areas where significant new learning has taken place? If you still have questions about some sections of the chapter, read them again. Check the glossary. You may want to discuss some of your questions with your instructor.

Step Eight: Suggestions for Further Observation and Study

1. Visit an elementary school. What are the strategies used to promote a sense of industry? What kinds of student achievements seem to receive the most public recognition?

2. Read the article by Eccles, J. S. (1993). School and family effects on the ontogeny of children's interests self-perceptions, and activity choices. In J. E. Jacobs (Ed.) <u>Nebraska Symposium on Motivation: 1992</u> (Vol 40, pp. 145-208). Lincoln: University of Nebraska Press. How do the social expectations of others, especially parents and teachers, influence one's own self-assessment and expectancies? What critical examples from your own experience can you identify in which your own assessment was substantially influenced, either positively or negatively, by what someone else thought you could accomplish?

3. Think back on your own experiences as a member of a team. What did you learn about yourself, about other team members, and about the norms of your community? Did you have any coaches that were especially memorable? What did they do that was supportive of you personal development or that of other team members; what did they do that might have interfered with your personal development or that of other team members? If your were to advise young children, what would you tell them about becoming involved in competitive, team experiences?

4. Look through recent popular periodicals for articles about how communities are dealing with violence in the schools. What are the basic controversies that arise in attempting to reduce violence? How are schools and communities attempting to resolve these controversies? How well are the developmental needs of children taken into account as schools and communities devise strategies to reduce violence?

CHAPTER NINE

Early Adolescence (12 to 18 Years)

Step One: Review the Chapter Outline

Developmental Tasks
    Physical Maturation
        Physical Changes in Girls
        Physical Changes in Boys
        The Secular Trend
        Individual Differences in Maturation Rate
    Formal Operations
        Piaget's Theory of Formal Operational Thought
        Six Characteristics of Formal Operational Thought
        Egocentrism
        Factors That Promote Formal Operational Thought
        Criticism of the Concept of Formal Operations
    Emotional Development
        Eating Disorders
        Delinquency
        Depression
    Membership in the Peer Group
        Cliques and Crowds
        Parents and Peers
    Sexual Relationships
        First Intercourse
        Sexual Orientation
        Problems and Conflicts Associated with Sexuality
        Parenthood in Early Adolescence
The Psychosocial Crisis: Group Identity versus Alienation
    Group Identity
    Alienation
The Central Process: Peer Pressure
    The Role of School Adults in Peer-Group Structuring
    Affiliating with a Peer Group
    Peer Pressure in Specific Areas
    Conformity and a Sense of Belonging
    Conflict, Tension, and Alienation
    Ethnic Group Identity
The Prime Adaptive Ego Quality and The Core Pathology
    Fidelity to Others
    Disassociation

Applied Topic: Adolescent Alcohol and Drug Use
  Factors Associated with Alcohol Use
End of Chapter Case

Step Two: Review the Chapter Objectives

9.1 To describe the patterns of physical maturation during puberty for males and females, including an analysis of the impact of early and late maturing self-concept and social relationships.

9.2 To introduce the basic features of formal operational reasoning, highlighting the new conceptual skills that emerge and factors that promote the development of formal operational thought.

9.3 To examine patterns of emotional development in early adolescence, including three examples of emotional disorders: eating disorders, delinquency, and depression.

9.4 To describe the further evolution of peer relations in early adolescence, especially the formation of cliques and crowds, and to contrast the impact of parents and peers during this stage.

9.5 To characterize the development of sexuality, with a special focus on the transition to coitus, the formation of a sexual orientation, and a detailed review of the factors associated with pregnancy and parenthood in adolescence.

9.6 To describe the psychosocial crisis of early adolescence, group identity versus alienation, and the central process through which the crisis is resolved, peer pressure, the prime adaptive ego quality of fidelity to others, and the core pathology – isolation.

9.7 To review the patterns of adolescent alcohol use and factors associated with alcohol abuse within a psychosocial framework.

Step Three: Take the Pre-Test

Answer these questions before you read the text. The pages where the material is discussed are indicated in the parentheses after each question. Use your performance as a guide to areas where you need to read especially carefully. The Answer Key for the pre-test can be found at the end of the study guide.

1. Which pattern best characterizes the physical changes associated with puberty? (pp. 304-308)
    a. They occur earlier for girls.
    b. They occur earlier for boys.
    c. They occur at the same time for boys and girls.
    d. They pose no problems for psychological development.

2. Which aspect of the physical changes of puberty concerns girls the most? (p. 306)
   a. the height spurt
   b. obesity
   c. breast development
   d. menstruation

3. Which one of the following is NOT a characteristic of formal operational thought? (pp. 310-312)
   a. more abstract thinking
   b. greater ability to think about the future
   c. greater ability to think about two or more variables at the same time
   d. greater reliance on sensory and motor experiences

4. Which of the following is an example of egocentrism in early adolescence? (pp. 312-313)
   a. Adolescents cannot separate actions from their effects.
   b. Adolescents cannot separate their perspective from that of the listener.
   c. Adolescents do not realize that others do not share their hypothetical construction of reality.
   d. Adolescents are selfish and do not value cooperation.

5. Symptoms of worrying, moodiness, crying, difficulty sleeping, and loss of interest in daily activities are associated with _____. (p. 319)
   a. anorexia nervosa
   b. delinquency
   c. egocentrism
   d. depression

6. Which statement best describes the nature of adolescent peer group relations? (pp.321-326)
   a. Peer group membership is important to only 10 percent of high school students.
   b. Peer group membership undermines the parent-child relationship.
   c. Peer groups become more structured and organized in early adolescence.
   d. Membership in a peer group is based primarily on academic ability.

7. The strongest predictor of early involvement in sexual activity is _____. (pp. 326-329)
   a. dating at an early age
   b. poor grades in school
   c. physical attractiveness
   d. watching sexual material on television

Chapter 9

8. Which of the following is the most important factor in determining how well an adolescent girl copes with pregnancy and motherhood? (pp. 332-335)
   a. how much she wanted to keep the baby
   b. the age at which the adolescent becomes pregnant
   c. the ease of childbirth
   d. whether her mother was pregnant in adolescence

9. The central process for resolving the psychosocial crisis of early adolescence is_____ . (pp. 338-340)
   a. education
   b. imitation
   c. trust
   d. peer pressure

10. What is the typical adolescent's view of binge drinking? (pp. 341-346)
    a. not very risky
    b. not very acceptable
    c. risky but acceptable
    d. risky and not acceptable

Step Four: Read Chapter 9: Early Adolescence

Step Five: Review Basic Concepts By Matching Each Term and Its Definition

a.	alienation	b.	anorexia nervosa
c.	egocentrism	d.	ethnic group identity
e.	formal operations	f.	group identity
g.	peer pressure	h.	puberty
i.	secular growth trend	j.	depression
k.	clique	l.	crowd

1. ( ) The period of physical development when the reproductive system matures.

2. ( ) A sense of isolation and separateness from others.

3. ( ) A tendency observed since approximately 1900 for earlier attainment of adult height and sexual maturation.

4. ( ) Expectations for conformity to group norms and sanctions for violation of norms.

5. ( ) In Piaget's theory, the final stage of cognitive development characterized by abstract reasoning, hypothesis generating, and hypothesis testing.

6. ( ) A disorder involving the inability to regulate eating behavior and a desire for extreme thinness.

7. ( ) A large group of peers characterized by similar patterns of behavior, shared values, and interlocking friendship.

8. ( ) A preoccupation with one's own logic and way of understanding experience.

9. ( ) A small friendship group of five to ten friends.

10. ( ) The positive pole of the psychosocial crisis of early adolescence in which the person finds membership in a peer group.

11. ( ) Feelings of sadness, loss of hope, and a sense of being overwhelmed by the demands of the world.

12. ( ) Realizing that some of one's thoughts, feelings, and beliefs are influenced by membership in a specific racial, religious, or cultural group.

Step Six: Answer the Focusing Questions

1. What kinds of psychological changes might be triggered by the physiological changes of puberty? (pp. 304-309)

2. How do males and females respond differently to the physical changes of puberty? (pp. 304-309)

3. What are six new conceptual skills that are associated with the acquisition of formal operational thought? (p. 311)

4. What are the key elements of emotional development that occur during early adolescence? (pp. 316-317)

5. What are the basic characteristics of Anorexia nervosa, Delinquency, and Depression? (pp. 317-321)

6. What are the consequences of parent-adolescent interaction for adolescent-peer relationships? (pp. 324-326)

_____

_____

_____

_____

Step Seven: Take the Post-Test

1. Which of the following best describes physical maturation for adolescent males? (pp. 307-308)
   a. includes increased height, weight and muscle mass
   b. occurs two years earlier than for females
   c. is characterized by a uniform growth rate in all body parts
   d. is usually accompanied by high levels of anxiety and dread

2. One consequence of the secular trend is that children _____. (p. 308)
   a. are more intelligent today than they were 100 years ago
   b. are shorter than they were in the past
   c. are more likely to be members of peer groups today than they were 100 years ago
   d. reach adult height earlier today than they did 100 years ago

3. Which of the following is a criticism of the concept of formal operational thought? (pp. 315-316)
   a. as children reach puberty, they all use formal reasoning
   b. formal reasoning is not necessary for solving most high school level tests
   c. formal reasoning is not a broad enough to construct to encompass all the dimensions along which cognitive functioning matures
   d. in modern times, adolescents don't like learning methods that require rote memorization

4. Which of the following is characteristic of anorexia nervosa? (pp. 317-318)
   a. flamboyance
   b. timidity and submissiveness
   c. aggressiveness
   d. no impulse control

Chapter 9

5. Of the following topics, which one is more likely to be a focus of adolescent-peer interactions than a focus of adolescent-parent interactions? (pp. 321-326)
    a. discipline and control
    b. friendships and peer relations
    c. academic goals and achievements
    d. career planning

6. In the transition to coitus, which of the following factors is associated with having a less permissive attitude toward premarital sex and a greater willingness to delay sexual activity? (pp. 326-329)
    a. early entry into puberty
    b. low academic aspirations
    c. strong religious values
    d. living in a step family

7. Which statement best describes the outcome for marriages involving adolescents who are pregnant? (pp. 331-335)
    a. They are stable and satisfying.
    b. They are three times more likely than other teenage marriages to end in divorce.
    c. They are less likely to de disrupted by poverty than most marriages.
    d. They have a better chance of surviving than teen marriages where the woman is not pregnant.

8. One likely outcome of alienation during early adolescence is that it _____. (pp. 336-338)
    a. provides a keen sense of group belonging
    b. prevents the development of a sense of industry
    c. creates uneasiness in the presence of peers
    d. increases understanding about peer pressure

9. A sense of ethnic group identity is heightened in early adolescence because _____. (pp. 339-340)
    a. adolescents encounter new sanctions against cross-race friendships and dating
    b. minority adolescents are highly valued within their peer group
    c. there are few differences in values between parents and peers
    d. the majority culture acknowledges the contributions of ethnic groups as part of its heritage

10. Which of the following is the most common explanation for why adults and adolescents use alcohol? (pp. 341-346)
    a. so they won't be different from their friends
    b. to add a feeling of festivity to social functions
    c. to help relieve pressure
    d. to create illusions of power

After completing the post-test, compare your score with your performance on the pre-test. Can you identify areas where significant new learning has taken place? If you still have questions about some sections of the chapter, read them again. Check the glossary. You may want to discuss some of your questions with your instructor.

Step Eight: Suggestions for Further Observation and Study

1. Make a list of the experiences in your own education that you believe have helped you to develop your formal operational reasoning skills. In which areas of intellectual functioning is your formal operational reasoning most fully developed? Why?

2. Think about your first date. Talk to friends, your parents or other middle adults about their early dating experiences. What are some common positive and negative experiences associated with these first dates? In what ways have the cultural norms about dating changed from your parents generation to your own? In what ways are early dating experiences opportunities for new learning about self and social relationships?

3. Why might adolescence be a time for heightened sensitivity around issues of ethnic identity? What are some examples of ways that members of an ethnic subculture might encounter conflicts with the predominant culture? What are some common strategies that adolescents use to cope with these conflicts?

4. Contact the director of an alcohol abuse prevention program or an alcohol abuse treatment program that focuses on youth. What are the primary components of these programs? How are the programs related to the psychosocial needs of early adolescents? How serious are problems associated with alcohol abuse among early adolescents in your community?

CHAPTER TEN

Later Adolescence (18 to 24 Years)

Step One: Review the Chapter Outline
Developmental Tasks
    Autonomy from Parents
        Autonomy and Leaving Home
        Autonomy and the College Experience
    Gender Identity
        The Role of Culture
        Gender-Linked Expectations
        A Reevaluation of Gender Constancy
        Learning New Sex-Role Standards and Reevaluating Old Ones
        Revising One's Childhood Identification
        Adding a Sexual Dimension to Gender Identity
        Finalizing Gender-Role Preference
    Internalized Morality
        New Cognitive Capacities
        Stages of Moral Reasoning
        Experiences that Promote Moral Reasoning
        Challenge to Kohlberg's View of Moral Reasoning
    Career Choice
        Work Experiences in Early Adolescence
        Factors Influencing Career Choice
        Rethinking the Concept of Career Choice
        Career Decision-Making
The Psychosocial Crisis: Individual Identity versus Identity Confusion
    The Content Component of Identity
    The Evaluation Component of Identity
    Identity Status
    Identity Formation for Males and Females
The Central Process: Role Experimentation
    Psychosocial Moratorium
    Role Experimentation and Ethnic Identity
The Prime Adaptive Ego Quality and The Core Pathology
    Fidelity to Values and Ideologies
    Repudiation
Applied Topic: Challenges of Social Life
    Unwanted Sexual Attention
    Binge Drinking
    Sexually Transmitted Diseases
End of Chapter Case

Step Two: Review the Chapter Objectives

10.1 To examine the concept of autonomy from parents and the conditions under which this autonomy is likely to be achieved.

10.2 To trace the development of gender identity in later adolescence, including a discussion of how the components of sex-role identification that were relevant during the early-school-age period are revised and expanded.

10.3 To describe the maturation of morality in later adolescence, with special focus on the role of new cognitive capacities that influence moral judgments and the various value orientations that underlie moral reasoning.

10.4 To analyze the process of career choice, with attention to education and gender-role socialization as two major influential factors.

10.5 To analyze the psychosocial crisis of later adolescence - individual identity versus identity confusion - the central process through which this crisis is resolved, role experimentation, the prime adaptive ego quality of values and ideals, and the core pathology of repudiation.

10.6 To examine some of the challenges of social life in later adolescence that may result in high-risk behaviors.

Step Three: Take the Pre-Test

Answer these questions <u>before</u> you read the text. The pages where the material is discussed are indicated in the parentheses after each question. Use your performance as a guide to areas where you need to read especially carefully. The Answer Key for the pre-test can be found at the end of the study guide.

1. Which of the following marks the psychological close of later adolescence? (pp. 349-383)
   a. getting married
   b. learning to drive a car
   c. having a child
   d. forming a personal identity

2. Which of the following best reflects autonomy from parents? (p. 351)
   a. total rejection of parents
   b. living in a separate home from parents
   c. children and parents accept one another's individuality
   d. alienation from parents

3. Which of the following terms refers to a set of beliefs, attitudes, and values about oneself as a man or a woman in many areas of social life? (p. 354)
   a. gender identity
   b. androgyny
   c. sex-role standards
   d. masculinity

4. Which is characteristic of postconventional moral reasoning? (p. 359)
   a. an awareness of the relativism of values
   b. concern for maintaining the existing rule structure
   c. concern about whether one's behaviors will be rewarded or punished
   d. concern about whether one's behaviors will benefit one's friends and family members

5. When faced with a moral dilemma, some people are especially concerned about how to arrive at a solution that will result in the least harm for all concerned. Which of the following refers to this kind of moral orientation? (pp. 360-361)
   a. prohibitive moral orientation
   b. caring orientation
   c. justice orientation
   d. utilitarian orientation

6. Which of the following is an example of how gender identity influences career choices? (p. 365)
   a. Men are more concerned about the status of their careers than woman.
   b. Men are more concerned about the interpersonal quality of instruction in their majors than woman.
   c. Women base their career decisions on their parents' careers.
   d. Feminine women are most likely to seek employment in male dominated fields.

7. What is the first phase in the career decision-making process? (pp. 367-369)
   a. crystallization
   b. choice
   c. exploration
   d. integration

8. The two structural components of identity are _____ and _____. (pp. 370-372)
   a. moratorium; mutuality
   b. content; evaluation
   c. congruence; androgyny
   d. positive; negative

9. Identity confusion refers to which of the following? (p. 373)
   a. premature decisions about identity
   b. commitment to values that are antagonistic to society
   c. commitment to parental values
   d. unintegrated roles and the absence of any commitment

Chapter 10

10. What is the central process for the resolution of the psychosocial crisis of individual identity versus identity confusion? (p. 375)
   a. postconventional reasoning
   b. moratorium
   c. role experimentation
   d. negative identity

Step Four: Read Chapter 10: Later Adolescence

Step Five: Review Basic Concepts by Matching Each Term and Its Definition

a.	prosocial moral judgements	b.	autonomy from parents
c.	identity achievement	d.	identity foreclosure
e.	internalized morality	f.	negative identity
g.	psychosocial moratorium	h.	identity confusion
i.	role experimentation	j.	gender identity
k.	crystallization phase	l.	induction phase

1. ( ) Identity status in which, after crisis, a sense of commitment to family, work, political, and religious values is established.

2. ( ) A period of free experimentation before individual identity is achieved.

3. ( ) The negative pole of the psychosocial crisis of later adolescence in which the person cannot make a commitment to any unified vision of the self.

4. ( ) An ability to regulate and guide one's behavior and make decisions without undue control from or dependence on one's parents.

5. ( ) Identity status in which commitments are established without questioning or crisis.

6. ( ) An integrated set of beliefs, attitudes, and values about oneself as a man or a woman in many areas of social life.

7. ( ) In career decision making, the time when costs and benefits of various alternatives are weighed and some alternative are discarded.

8. ( ) Moral decisions involving a conflict between doing something helpful for someone else and doing something to meet one's own needs.

9. ( ) A set of values, beliefs, and ethical principles that guide behavior.

10. ( ) A clearly defined self-image that is contrary to the cultural values of the community.

11. ( ) In career decision making, when a person enters the new work environment for the first time makes efforts to be recognized and accepted.

12. ( ) Participation in a variety of roles as a means of discovering one's role commitments.

Step Six: Answer the Focusing Questions

1. How might the college experience influence the achievement of autonomy from parents? (pp. 351-353)

   _____
   _____
   _____
   _____

2. Explain how culture influences gender identity through its impact on sex-role standards; the expression of sexual impulses; and sex-role preferences. (pp. 354-358)

   _____
   _____
   _____
   _____

3. What are three challenges to Kohlberg's view of moral development? (pp.358-362)

   _____
   _____
   _____
   _____

4. How are gender socialization and career choice related? (pp.362-369)

_____

_____

_____

_____

5. Define each of the five identity statuses: achievement, foreclosure, moratorium, identity confusion, and negative identity. (pp. 372-374)

_____

_____

_____

_____

6. In your words, describe the process of career choice and explain how current changes in the labor market might effect career choice in later adolescence. (p. 369; pp. 375-379)

_____

_____

_____

_____

Step Seven: Take the Post-Test

1. How can parents assist their children in becoming comfortably independent in later adolescence? (pp. 351-353)
    a. allow children to contribute to decision making
    b. best firm limits and never budge from them
    c. never explain why rules are made
    d. become preoccupied with their own careers

2. From 1970 to 1991, what has changed in the pattern of 18- to 24-year-olds who live in their parents' household? (p. 352)
   a. A smaller percent live in their parents' household in 1991 than in 1970.
   b. A larger percent live in their parents household in 1991 than in 1970.
   c. More females live in their parents' household in 1991, whereas more males live alone.
   d. In 1991, the majority of 18-24-year olds were married and living in their own households, whereas in 1970 the majority were living by themselves.

3. Which term refers to cultural expectations concerning the appropriate behavior for males and females? (p. 355)
   a. gender constancy
   b. identification
   c. sex-role preference
   d. sex-role standards

4. Research on Kohlberg's theory of moral development finds that _____. (p. 359)
   a. there is no stage-like progression in moral reasoning
   b. conventional reasoning is the earliest form of moral
   c. individuals cannot follow arguments about moral issues unless they are presented at exactly their own level of moral judgement
   d. the sequence of stages from 1 through 4 is observed in many different societies

5. Which of the following is a prosocial moral judgement? (p. 360)
   a. deciding to steal or let someone die
   b. deciding to lie or hurt someone's feelings
   c. deciding to forge a signature or let someone suffer
   d. deciding to give directions to someone who is lost even though it will make you late for an appointment

6. Which factor do high school and college students say plays the greatest role in their career decision making? (p. 362)
   a. individual factors (talents, abilities)
   b. socioeconomic factors (social class, race)
   c. family factors (mother and father as role models)
   d. societal factors (education, mass media)

7. Which of the following statements best characterizes Tiedman's model of career decision making? (pp.367-369)
    a. Career decisions are based primarily on external rewards.
    b. Men make more logical decisions about careers than do women.
    c. Career decision making involves continuous interaction between the individual and the work context.
    d. The first phases of career decision making can be bypassed for those who have a college degree.

8. Which of the following is an example of a characteristic of the current labor market that is relevant for career-decision-making? (p. 369)
    a. There are fewer are kinds of jobs today than in the past.
    b. Companies are in a period of expansion with many new management level positions being established each year.
    c. New careers emerge at a rapid pace as new technologies arise and new roles are required to link various kinds of work.
    d. There are few opportunities to change career directions over the course of one's occupational lifetime.

9. What criteria does James Marcia use to determine a person's identity status? (p. 372)
    a. the experience of crisis
    b. commitment to values
    c. alienation from the peer group
    d. a combination of a and b

10. Which of the statements about identity formation is true? (pp. 372-374)
    a. Identity achievement is associated with positive ego qualities for men but not for women.
    b. Moratorium is a more anxiety-filled status for women than for men.
    c. Vocational commitments are more central to the identity content for women than for men.
    d. Men who have a foreclosed identity are flexible and optimistic.

After completing the post-test, compare your score with your performance on the pre-test. Can you identify areas where significant new learning has taken place? If you still have questions about sections of the chapter, read them again. Check the glossary. You may want to discuss some of your questions with your instructor.

Step Eight: Suggestions for Further Observation and Study

1. Analyze the extent of your autonomy from your parents. In what areas are you still dependent on them? What evidence do you have that they view you in a more autonomous light than they did during your early adolescence?

2. What aspects of United States culture make it difficult to develop a clear sense of individual identity? Read Erik Erikson's Identity: Youth and Crisis, New York: W. W. Norton, 1968. How would you compare the emphasis on the development of individual identity in the United States with the emphasis in specific other cultures?

3. Investigate the availability of career-decision-making resources at your college or university. How are issues of gender identity, moral values, and relationships with parents addressed in career development materials?

4. In what ways does the college environment stimulate your own work on identity formation? Examine each content area - vocational goals and values, interpersonal relations, political ideology, religious/moral values, values regarding family roles. In what ways do experiences in and outside of class have an impact on your experience of crisis or commitment in each of these areas?

CHAPTER ELEVEN

Early Adulthood (24 to 34 Years)

Step One: Review the Chapter Outline

Major Concepts in the Study of Adulthood
    Social Roles
    Social Clock
    Life Course
    Functional Autonomy of Motives
    Tendencies toward Growth
Developmental Tasks
    Exploring Intimate Relationships
        Readiness to Marry
        Selection of a Partner
        Adjustment During the Early Years of Marriage
        Adjustment in Dual-Earner Marriages
    Childbearing
        The Impact of Childbearing on Marriage
        The Decision Not to Have Children
    Work
        Technical Skills
        Authority Relations
        Demands and Hazards
        Interpersonal Relationships with Co-Workers
        Career Opportunities
    Lifestyle
        Pace of Life
        Investment in Work
        Social Network
        Competing Role Demands
        Health and Fitness
        The Single Lifestyle
The Psychosocial Crisis: Intimacy versus Isolation
    Intimacy

                Isolation
                    Loneliness
                    Depression
                    Fragile Identity
                    Sexual Disorders
                    Situational Factors
                    Divergent Spheres of Interest
                    Enmeshment
        The Central Process: Mutuality Among Peers
            Love
            Exclusivity
        Applied Topic: Divorce
            Factors Contributing to Divorce
            Coping with Divorce
        End of Chapter Case

Step Two: Review the Chapter Objectives

11.1 To identify selected concepts that are especially relevant for understanding development during adulthood including life roles, the social clock, the life course, functional autonomy of motives, and tendencies toward growth.

11.2 To analyze the process of forming intimate relationships, including identifying and committing to a long-term relationship, the role of cohabitation in forming close relationships, and the challenges one faces in adjusting to the early years of marriage.

11.3 To describe factors associated with the decision to have children, the impact of childbearing on the intimate, parental relationship, and the contribution of childbearing to growth in adulthood.

11.4 To explore the concept of work as a stimulus for psychological development in early adulthood with special focus on the technical skills, authority relations, demands and hazards, and interpersonal relations of the work environment.

11.5 To examine the concept of lifestyle as the expression of individual identity, with consideration of single lifestyles.

11.6 To define and describe the psychosocial crisis of early adulthood - intimacy versus isolation; the central process through which the crisis: mutuality among peers; the prime adaptive ego quality of love; and the core pathology of exclusivity.

11.7 To analyze divorce as a life stressor in early adulthood including factors contributing to divorce and the coping process.

Step Three: Take the Pre-Test

Answer these questions before you read the text. The pages where the material is discussed are indicated in the parentheses after each question. Use your performance as a guide to areas where you need to read especially carefully. The Answer Key for the pre-test can be found at the end of the study guide.

1. What happens during adulthood with respect to life roles? (pp. 386-387)
    a. The number of roles increases.
    b. The number of roles decreases.
    c. The number of roles remains constant throughout adolescence and adulthood.
    d. Roles become less demanding.

2. Which of the following best describes the functional autonomy of motives? (p. 389)
    a. Motives are fixed and unchangeable.
    b. Motives are unconscious.
    c. Motives are determined in childhood.
    d. Motives are flexible and open to change.

3. Which of the following factors determines whether an initial attraction between two people will move into a deeper attraction? (pp. 392-394)
    a. The couple take a vacation together.
    b. The couple disclose information about themselves that reveals basic similarities.
    c. The couple argue over values.
    d. The couple begin to date other people.

4. Which of the following statements about communication in marriage is true? (pp. 401-403)
    a. Happy couples and distressed couples have about the same amount of negative interactions.
    b. Husbands who are emotionally expressive contribute to higher levels of conflict in marriage.
    c. Happy couples are better able to limit expressions of hostility than distressed couples.
    d. Distressed couples and happy couples use the same strategies to resolve conflict.

5. Which of the following is likely to occur after the birth of the first child? (pp. 404-408)
    a. monetary resources increase
    b. greater sexual intimacy
    c. lower marital satisfaction
    d. less role strain

6. Approximately what percent of married women aged 18 to 34 do NOT expect to have children? (p. 408)
   a. 5%
   b. 10%
   c. 15%
   d. 20%

7. Which of the following characterizes the work experiences of early adulthood? (pp. 409-413)
   a. training
   b. management
   c. expansion of authority
   d. retirement planning

8. For most people, establishing a lifestyle requires balancing _____.
   (pp. 413-417)
   a. the checkbook
   b. anxiety and depression
   c. time alone and time with others
   d. role demands

9. Which of the following terms refer to the ability to experience an open, supportive, tender relationship with another person, without fear of losing one's own identity? (p. 417)
   a. integrity
   b. intimacy
   c. commitment
   d. passion

10. Which of the following statements about coping with divorce is true? (pp. 426-427)
    a. Divorced people are likely to retain an attachment to their former spouse which interferes with adjustment.
    b. Divorced people are no different from those people who are married and never divorced with respect to life satisfaction.
    c. Divorced people readily become involved in a new set of adult social relationship.
    d. Expressing your feelings appears to be one of the most effective ways of coping with the stress of divorce.

Step Four: Read Chapter 11: Early Adulthood

Step Five: Review Basic Concepts by Matching Each Term and Its Definition

a.	dual-earner marriage	b.	intimacy
c.	life course	d.	functional autonomy of motives
e.	isolation	f.	tendencies toward growth
g.	occupational hazards	h.	mutuality
i.	social clock	j.	enmeshment
k.	lifestyle	l.	social integration

1. ( ) A relatively permanent structure of activity, including the tempo of activity, the balance between work and leisure, and patterns of family and social relationships.

2. ( ) Social expectations for changes in roles and responsibilities that are tied to age norms.

3. ( ) In Allport's theory, the idea that behaviors may initially be performed because of a specific motive, but may continue because of the enjoyment they bring or the new resources they provide.

4. ( ) Married couples both of whom participate in the labor force.

5. ( ) A crisis resolution in which a person remains psychologically distant from others.

6. ( ) The ability to experience an open, supportive, tender relationship with another person, without the fear of losing one's own identity.

7. ( ) In White's theory, five areas of new development leading to maturity into adulthood.

8. ( ) The pattern of significant roles, events, and transitions a person experiences from infancy through later adulthood.

9. ( ) The degree to which people are connected to others in the community especially through a shared value system.

10. ( ) The ability of two people to meet each other's needs.

11. ( ) Physical and psychological risks associated with the workplace.

12. ( ) Relationships characterized by over-involvement and strong resistance to any change by either partner.

Step Six: Answer the Focusing Questions

1. What are the five tendencies toward growth in Robert White's theory? Give an example of a situation that produces growth in each area. (pp. 390-392)

2. What are the four phases in the mate selection process? What factors determine whether the relationship moves along or terminates? (pp. 394-398)

3. What are the major sources of stress in dual-career marriages? (pp. 403-404)

4. What is the impact of the birth of a child on the marriage relationship? (pp. 404-409)

5. How might the work setting stimulate new learning in early adulthood? (pp. 409-413)

6. What are four factors that influence the formation of one's lifestyle in early adulthood? (pp. 413-417)

7. What factors in the socialization of men and women pose barriers to the achievement of intimacy? (pp. 417-419)

8. Discuss factors that account for divorce from national, community, and couple levels of analysis. (pp. 423-426)

_____

_____

_____

_____

Step Seven: Take the Post-Test

1. Which of the following is NOT mentioned by White as one of the tendencies toward growth in adulthood? (pp. 390-392)
   a. freeing of personal relationships
   b. deepening of interests
   c. strengthening of defenses
   d. humanizing of values

2. Often, the decision to marry is a response to _____. (pp. 393-394)
   a. fluctuations in self-esteem
   b. the social clock
   c. moral judgements
   d. needs for autonomy

3. Which of the following factors plays a part in moving a couple from phase III, deep attraction, to phase IV, "the right one" relationship? (pp. 394-398)
   a. potential loss of a confidante and companion
   b. differences in interest
   c. negative self-disclosure
   d. physical attraction

4. High-quality, dual-career marriages are likely to be characterized by _____. (pp. 403-404)
   a. the presence of preschool-age children
   b. careers in traditional businesses such as law or accounting
   c. wives earnings more than husbands
   d. role sharing and companionship

5. In a national survey, what was the most important benefit associated with having children for both men and women? (p. 405)
   a. having someone to care for them in old age
   b. fulfilling one's religious duties
   c. having someone to love
   d. completing one's marriage

6. Which of the following is NOT discussed as a central component of the occupational search and training period? (pp. 409-413)
   a. authority relations
   b. technical skills
   c. interpersonal relations with peers
   d. emotional expressiveness

7. Which of the following is an extrinsic factor influencing job choice? (pp. 409-413)
   a. interest in the job
   b. financial pressures form the family
   c. responsibility on the job
   d. opportunities for advancement

8. Which of the following statements regarding the single lifestyle is true? (pp. 415-417)
   a. Many single people live with family members or roommates.
   b. Singles who have never married are very lonely.
   c. Highly educated women are more likely to see disadvantages in being single.
   d. Singles have a higher frequency of sexual activity than married couples.

9. According to research evidence, which of the following relationships is likely to be least intimate? (pp. 417-418)
   a. two men
   b. two women
   c. a man and a woman
   d. a married couple

10. How is one's family history of divorce related to the likelihood of divorcing as an adult? (pp. 425-426)
    a. There is no relationship between experiencing parents' divorce as a child and divorcing as an adult.
    b. Those who experience their parents' divorce as children are less likely to divorce as adults.
    c. Those who experience their parents' divorce as children are more likely to divorce as adults.
    d. Women who experience their parents' divorce as children are more likely to divorce as adults: this is not true for men.

After completing the post-test, compare your score with your performance on the pre-test. Can you identify areas where significant new learning has taken place? If you still have questions of the chapter, read them again. Check the glossary. You may want to discuss some of your questions with your instructor.

Step Eight: Suggestions for Further Observation and Study

1. Using Figure 11.1 on page 389 as a guide, map your own life course.. Include more details about events that have influenced the direction of your occupational career and your family career.

2. Trace the history of your most recent intimate relationship using Figure 11.3 on page 359 as a guide. What factors were associated with the initial attraction? How far did the relationship progress (i.e. Phase II, III, IV). What factors were involved in moving the relationship to the next phase or in terminating the relationship? In general, how useful is this model for understanding the history of a real-life example?

3. Think about your own plans for career and family. In what areas do you anticipate role conflict? In what areas do you expect role complementarity?

4. Read further about the differences between men and women in their need for intimate relationships. One very interesting source is Tanner, D. You just don't understand: Men and women in conversation. New York: William Morrow, 1990. What are some of the socialization practices that account for these differences? Are there cultural examples of societies that succeed in developing greater compatibility between men and women along this dimension than our own?

5. Visit with an attorney or a judge who deals with divorce. Then visit with a marriage and family therapist who works with couples going through divorce. Contrast their views. What are the primary reasons for divorce? What steps do they think couples could take to prevent divorce? What resources are available in your community to assist couples who are experiences serious marital conflict?

CHAPTER TWELVE

Middle Adulthood (34-60 Years)

Step One: Review the Chapter Outline

Developmental Tasks
    Managing a Career
        Achieving New Levels of Competence in the World of Work
        Midlife Career Changes
        Work and Family Life
        The Impact of Joblessness
    Nurturing an Intimate Relationship
        A Commitment to Growth
        Effective Communication
        Creative Use of Conflict
    Expanding Caring Relationships
        Parenting
        Caring for One's Aging Parents
    Managing the Household
        Building Coalitions
        One-Parent Families
        People Who Live Alone
The Psychosocial Crisis: Generativity Versus Stagnation
    Generativity
        Measuring Generativity
    Stagnation
The Central Process: Person-Environment Interaction and Creativity
    Person-Environment Interaction
    Creativity
The Prime Adaptive Ego Quality and the Core Pathology
    Care
    Rejectivity
Applied Topic: Discrimination in the Workplace
    Disparities in Income and Occupational Structure
    How Discrimination Perpetuates Itself
    Psychosocial Analysis: Discrimination and Coping
End of Chapter Case

Step Two: Review the Chapter Objectives

12.1 To examine the world of work as a context for development, focusing on interpersonal demands, authority relations, and demands for acquisition of new skills, considering the interaction of work and family life, and examining the impact of joblessness in middle adulthood.

12.2 To examine the process of maintaining a vital intimate relationship in middle adulthood, especially a commitment to growth, effective communication, and creative use of conflict.

12.3 To describe the expansion of caring in middle adulthood as it applies to two specific roles: that of parent and that of adult child caring for one's aging parents.

12.4 To analyze the broad range of tasks required for the effective management of the household for their impact on cognitive, social, and emotional development of family members.

12.5 To explain the psychosocial crisis of generativity versus stagnation and the central process through which the crisis is resolved: person-environment interaction and creativity. To define the primary ego strength of care and the core pathology of rejectivity.

12.6 To apply a psychosocial analysis to the issue of discrimination in the workplace with special focus on the cost to society as well as to the individual when discrimination operates to restrict career access and advancement.

Step Three: Take the Pre-Test

Answer these questions before you read the text. The pages where material is discussed are indicated in the parentheses after each question. Use your performance as a guide to areas where you need to read especially carefully. The Answer Key for the pre-test can be found at the end of the study guide.

1. Career advancement, generally requires that an individual has a willingness to assume new levels of _____. (p. 433)
   a. subordination
   b. discrimination in occupational structure
   c. authority and responsibility
   d. exposure to physical and mental hazards

2. Which of the following is a characteristic of a vital marriage? (pp. 440-441)
   a. The couple is committed to individual and couple growth.
   b. Communication is not needed because so much is already understood.
   c. Conflict is avoided.
   d. Levels of complaining and negative communication increase.

3. Which of the following statements best describes the relationship between parents and children? (p. 443)
   a. Children have no influence on a parent's development.
   b. Parents have no influence on a child's development.
   c. Children help parents learn about parenting based on their responses to parenting efforts.
   d. Parents help children by keeping the same demands on child ignoring the child's developmental level.

4. During middle adulthood, one's capacity to be generative can be determined through an adult's commitment to _____. (p. 449)
   a. aging parents
   b. grandchildren
   c. children
   d. all of the these

5. Among couples who are happily married and are parents, what is most likely to happen after their children grow up and leave home? (pp. 445-446)
   a. increased marital conflict
   b. boredom in the relationship
   c. increased togetherness as a couple
   d. depression over the loss of the parent role

6. Regina's parents are older and are beginning to have problems performing some basic household tasks. Regina prioritizes helping her parents and feels a sense of duty to assist them whenever she is able. This is an example of _____. (p. 450)
   a. fear of stagnation
   b. rejectivity
   c. filial obligation
   d. parental authority

7. Managing a household is a developmental task of middle adulthood and is compared to _____. (p. 453)
   a. leadership skills in a paid work environment
   b. a sense of industry
   c. a need to fulfill family roles
   d. an outlet for stress relief

8. Which of the following best describes generativity? (p. 456)
   a. an ability to self disclose in an intimate relationship
   b. a commitment to improving societal conditions for future generations
   c. an integration of past core pathologies with current goals
   d. a commitment to skill development and career advancement

9. Which of the following groups of people would you characterize as achieving a sense of stagnation? (p. 458)
   a. people who live alone
   b. single parents
   c. chronically depressed people
   d. caregivers

10. Which of the following reflects job discrimination? People are selected for a job based on_____. (p. 465)
    a. past experience in similar work
    b. their membership in a specific group
    c. how much training they have had
    d. their performance on a job-related test

Step Four: Read Chapter 12: Middle Adulthood

Step Five: Review Basic Concepts By Matching Each Term and Its Definition

a. generativity   b. stagnation
c. discrimination   d. creativity
e. management of the household   f. career management
g. person-environment interaction h. vital marriage
i. filial obligation

1. ( )   The willingness to abandon old forms or patterns and to think in new ways.

2. ( )   A relationship in which there is strong commitment in which there is an enduring marital dyad in which each person experiences increasing fulfillment and satisfaction.

3. ( )   A range of administrative skills that have as their focus the enhancement of the home environment.

4. ( )   A child's sense of responsibility for the care and support of his/her parents.

5. ( ) A process of reciprocal influence between individual needs, talents, and resources, and the opportunities and demands of social and physical settings.

6. ( ) Decisions about a person, based on that person's membership in a group rather than on the person's competence and merit.

7. ( ) A lack of psychological movement or growth which results from self-aggrandizement or from the inability to cope with developmental tasks.

8. ( ) The desire to improve the quality of life for future generations.

9. ( ) An understanding of leadership and authority which allows for the expansion of interpersonal skills, the meeting of new skills demands with an achievement of mastery.

Step Six: Answer the Focusing Questions

1. What are the four major developmental tasks associated with middle adulthood? (pp. 432-433)

2. What are the major challenges in managing a career in middle adulthood? (pp. 433-440)

3. Apply the strains of job loss to the psychosocial crisis of generativity versus stagnation. (pp. 439-440)

4. List and briefly explain the three requirements for maintaining a vital marriage. (pp. 440-443)

4. Expanding caring relationships is a developmental task of middle adulthood. Explain how parenting and how caring for an aging parent contributes to adult development. (pp. 443-452)

5. Creativity is a process associated with generativity. For each of the following household management tasks, provide an example of creative problem solving and relate how each tasks helps an individual achieve generativity. (pp. 452-456; 460-462)

6. Describe an individual who has achieved a sense of generativity. (pp. 456-458)

7. Describe an individual who has achieved a sense of stagnation. (pp. 458-459)

8. List and explain the factors that account for race, ethnic, and gender discrimination in the workplace. (pp. 463-466)

Chapter 12

Step Seven: Take the Post-Test

1. Which of the following descriptors best captures the essence of generativity? (p. 430)
   a. self absorption, career-driven
   b. organized, work-alcoholic
   c. self-centered, uncaring
   d. peaceful, hopeful

2. During middle adulthood, which of the following changes is expected to occur? (p. 432)
   a. a decreased emphasis on intellectual attainment
   b. more focus on nurturing relationships
   c. greater concern about peer approval
   d. less openness about oneself

3. Which of the following is a characteristic of harmonious, satisfied marriage partners? (p. 442)
   a. a higher level of complaints
   b. an avoidance of verbal and non verbal interactions
   c. consideration of each other's problems
   d. an inability to listen to each other

4. Which of the following statements best describes the contributions of parenting to adult development? (p. 448)
   a. Parenting makes a very small contribution to an adult's development.
   b. Parenthood helps adults realize their progress in terms of self-identification.
   c. Parenting has a significant impact on adult development only when the children have left the home.
   d. Parenthood is a stage that makes no contribution to an adult's development.

5. Filial obligation is _____. (p. 450)
   a. an ability to redefine family obligations and norms in new ways
   b. a child's sense of responsibility to his/her parents
   c. perceived duty by a parent to care for one's children
   d. an ability to understand a child's developmental levels

6. Which of the following is NOT considered a contributing factor to the increased number of families with children who are homeless? (p. 452)
   a. kinship support
   b. joblessness of parents
   c. domestic violence focusing on the wife/mother only
   d. living in a rural area

7. If an individual has a sense of generative concern, then he/she typically _____. (p. 457)
   a. has narcissistic tendencies
   b. is not able to fulfill filial obligations
   c. is self-absorbed with career goals
   d. is satisfied with life

8. Grover created several paintings and developed training manuals in order to leave something tangible behind in order for his children, Zoe and Elmo, to take over various family obligations. What theme of generativity does this best describe? (p. 458)
   a. productivity
   b. caring
   c. general generativity
   d. grand generativity

9. Which of the following statements best applies to creativity in terms of achieving a sense of generativity? (pp. 461-462)
   a. Creativity is a random outlet with little focus needed.
   b. Creativity requires the middle adult to maintain control over all aspects of life.
   c. Creativity requires deliberate attention to be fostered.
   d. Creativity is a direct result of narcissistic individuals.

10. Rejectivity refers to _____. (p. 463)
    a. an individual's ego strength
    b. an unwillingness to accept certain individuals
    c. a need to interact with various environments to be accepted
    d. a basis for discrimination in the workplace

After completing the post-test, compare your score with your performance on the pre-test. Can you identify areas where significant new learning has taken place? If you still have questions about sections of the chapter, read them again. You may want to discuss some of your questions with your instructor.

Step Eight: Suggestions for Further Observation and Study

1. Talk to your parents about their perceptions of middle adulthood. What challenges are they facing? What challenges did they face? What are or were the major sources of satisfaction for them during middle adulthood?

2. Make a career and family life line. Plot your previous career achievements and major family life events. Plan your future achievements and major events. At what ages have career and family been in conflict? At what ages will career and family be in conflict? How will these conflicts impact the achievement of generativity?

3. Explore various web-sites focusing on the caregiving of elderly parents. Log-in to various 'chat rooms' developed for adult children caring for their elderly parents. What are the major concerns? How do these concerns apply to the psychosocial crisis of generativity versus stagnation?

4. Families are unique and are associated with many lifestyles. In this chapter and previous chapters, various family lifestyles have been examined, such as the single lifestyle, dual-career couples, childless couples, single-parent families, gay and lesbian parents, and families with various cultural value systems. Select one or two of these lifestyles. Identify some of the difficulties or benefits individuals from these pluralistic lifestyles would have for resolving the psychosocial crisis of generativity versus stagnation.

5. As you age, you experience various relationship changes with your parents. What sorts of changes are likely to occur in the near future? What sorts of changes are likely to occur as you age, particularly during middle adulthood? What is the ideal relationship you would like to have with your parents? How is generativity or stagnation embedded in this ideal relationship?

6. Examine a previous workplace. What evidence, if any, was there for discrimination in hiring practices, opportunities for promotion, or systematic differences in salaries, benefits, and annual raises? What programs, policies, and practices were in place to prevent or reduce discrimination at that workplace?

7. Examine a future workplace, based on your intended career goal. What evidence would you look for during an interview process for discrimination practices? What questions will you ask to determine the programs, policies, and practices that discourage discrimination? Are these issues important to you? If yes, then ask yourself why. If no, then also ask yourself why.

CHAPTER THIRTEEN

Later Adulthood (60-75 Years)

Step One: Review the Chapter Outline

Developmental Tasks
    Promoting Intellectual Vigor
        Problems in Defining and Studying Intelligence in Later Adulthood
        Productivity in the Work Setting
        Memory
        Piagetian Tasks
        Practical Problem Solving
        Patterns of Change in Different Mental Abilities
        The Interaction of Heredity and Environment on Mental Functioning
    Redirecting Energy to New Roles and Activities
        Grandparenthood
            Grandparent Caregivers
            Loss of Grandparent-Grandchild Contact
        Widowhood
            Widows
            Widowers
        Leisure Activities
    Accepting One's Life
        Illness and Health
        Life Satisfaction
        Subjective Age and Satisfaction
        Life Goals and Satisfaction
        Personality and Well-Being
    Developing a Point of View about Death
        Changing Perspectives about Death
        Death Anxiety
        Grief and Bereavement
        Death-Related Rituals
        A Cultural Comparison
        The Right to Die
The Psychosocial Crisis: Integrity versus Despair
    Integrity
    Despair
        Depression
The Central Process: Introspection

The Prime Adaptive Ego Quality and the Core Pathology
> Wisdom
> Disdain

Applied Topic: Retirement
> Adjustment to Retirement
>> Planning for Retirement
>> Perceptions of Retirement
>> Income Loss
> A Look Toward the Future of Retirement

Chapter Summary
End of Chapter Case

Step Two: Review the Chapter Objectives

13.1 To describe factors that promote intellectual vigor during later adulthood with a focus on the areas of cognitive functioning that have been studied including productivity in the workplace, memory, Piagetian-type tasks, and practical problem solving.

13.2 To examine the process of redirecting energy to new roles and activities with special focus on the role gain, such as grandparenthood; role loss, such as widowhood; and new opportunities for leisure.

13.3 To explore the construct of life satisfaction in later adulthood and factors associated with subjective well-being.

13.4 To describe the development of a point of view about death as a major psychological task of later adulthood.

13.5 To explain the psychosocial crisis of integrity versus despair, the central process of introspection, the prime adaptive ego quality of wisdom, and the core pathology of disdain.

13.6 To apply theory and research to understanding the process of adjustment to retirement in later adulthood.

Step Three: Take the Pre-Test

Answer these questions before you read the text. The pages where material is discussed are indicated in the parentheses after each question. Use your performance as a guide to areas where you need to read especially carefully. The Answer Key for the pre-test can be found at the end of the study guide.

1. The integrating theme of life in later adulthood is _____. (p. 470)
   a. a search for personal meaning.
   b. a sense of industry.
   c. a search for identity.
   d. a longing for intimacy.

2. When thinking about continued development in later adulthood, one must keep in mind individual differences in _____. (p. 470)
   a. life expectancy
   b. integrity
   c. physical and mental health
   d. work environment

3. A common worry among older adults is _____. (p. 473)
   a. a concern about loss of memory
   b. the inability to solve problems involving concrete operational reasoning
   c. a decline in crystallized intelligence
   d. a decline in fluid intelligence

4. Widowhood and retirement are two examples of _____. (p. 477)
   a. role boundaries
   b. role gain
   c. role loss
   d. role spillover

5. Which of the following is an event that commonly stimulates thoughts about death in middle adulthood? (p. 488)
   a. the death of a sibling
   b. the death of one's parents
   c. a near death experience
   d. birth of a child

6. The fear associated with being in pain, fear, and having others see you suffer is related to which of the following concepts? (p. 491)
   a. concerns about the social consequences of dying
   b. concerns about integrity
   c. concerns about despair
   d. concerns about the process of dying

7. What is one consequence associated with achieving a sense of integrity? (p. 494)
   a. the ability to face death without fear
   b. the ability to act decisively
   c. the ability to have an impact on others
   d. the ability to predict future events

8. What is the meaning of despair? (p. 494)
   a. conflict between competing roles of work and retirement
   b. discouragement about the past and a wish to do things differently
   c. a sense of loneliness and separateness from others
   d. a mistrust of others

9. Which of the following is NOT a factor which influences the adjustment to retirement? (p. 498)
   a. planning
   b. perception of retirement
   c. the degree of income loss
   d. the degree of generative concern

10. The ability to look back on one's life and achievements with satisfaction promotes _____. (p. 501)
    a. a sense of wisdom
    b. fluid intelligence
    c. the financial ability to retire
    d. an unacceptable reality about one's life

Step Four: Read Chapter 13: Later Adulthood

Step Five: Review Basic Concepts by Matching Each Terms and Its Definition

a. integrity   b. despair
c. wisdom   d. disdain
e. cohort   f. retirement
g. crystallized intelligence   h. fluid intelligence
i. introspection   j. reminiscence
k. bereavement

1. ( )   The emotional suffering following the death of a loved one.

2. ( )   A feeling of scorn for the weakness of oneself and others.

3. ( )   The ability to bring knowledge gained through past experience into play in appropriate situations.

4. ( )   Deliberate self-evaluation and review of thoughts and feelings.

5. ( )   The psychological state of withdrawal from one's work and a new orientation towards work.

6. ( )   People born during the same historical period.

7. ( )   Detached, yet active concern with life itself in the face of death.

8. ( )   The ability to impose organization on information and to generate new hypotheses.

9. ( )   Feeling of loss of all hope and confidence.

10. ( )   The ability to accept the facts of one's life and to face death without great fears.

11. ( )   The process of thinking or telling about past experiences.

Step Six: Answer the Focusing Questions

1. What are the four major developmental tasks associated with later adulthood? (p. 471)

2. List four problems that make it difficult to study intelligence in later life. (p. 471-472)

3. What are some suggestions you would give to an older adult for promoting optimal intellectual functioning? (p. 477)

4. In what ways do grandparenthood and widowhood allow for the redirection of energy in later adulthood? (p. 477-482)

5. What are the primary benefits of leisure activities for older adults? (p. 482-483)

6. In what ways do older adults differ from individuals in early and middle adulthood with respect to their point of view about death? (p. 488-490)

7. How does the process of introspection help older adults resolve the psychosocial crisis of integrity versus despair? (pp. 495-497)

8. What are the basic features of wisdom? (p. 497)

9. How is coping with retirement related to the developmental tasks of later adulthood? (pp. 498-501)

Step Seven: Take the Post-Test

1. Which of the following is NOT a developmental task of later adulthood? (p. 471)
    a. acceptance of one's life
    b. developing a point of view about death
    c. redirecting energy to new roles
    d. disengagement from intellectual activity

2. In later adulthood, which type of memory is most affected by the aging process? (pp. 472-473)
    a. short term memory
    b. long term memory
    c. semantic memory
    d. childhood memory

3. In the discussion of redirection of energy to new roles, three examples were given. Which roles or activity was NOT included? (p. 477)
    a. grandparenthood
    b. widowhood
    c. leisure activities
    d. political activist

4. Identifying with the label "old" is associated with which of the following for older adults? (p. 486)
   a. integrity
   b. self-esteem
   c. unemployment
   d. difficulty adjusting to life

5. Which of the following is NOT an explanation for the decrease in death anxiety for older adults? (pp. 490-491)
   a. older people have less experience with death than younger adults
   b. older people tend to be more religious and find comfort in the concept of death
   c. older people may feel more accepting of their lives and decisions they have made
   d. older people are more familiar with death

6. One can conclude that introspection is _____. (p. 495)
   a. totally objective.
   b. limited to memories of the past ten years.
   c. a process that usually leads to despair.
   d. a process that fosters a sense of continuity for older adults.

7. Pauline has regret about her past and a nagging wish to have done things differently, especially concerning her education and professional career. Pauline can be characterized as having a sense of _____. (p. 494)
   a. wisdom
   b. stagnation
   c. despair
   d. role confusion

8. Which of the following terms refers to the process of deliberate self-evaluation linked to the ability to achieve integrity? (p. 495)
   a. introspection
   b. crystallized intelligence
   c. social support
   d. identification

9. The capacity of older adults to attain wisdom is important for _____. (p. 497)
   a. the achievement of trust in infancy
   b. the preparation of retirement
   c. the continuation of society
   d. role transition to widowhood

10. The adjustment to retirement tends to be more difficult due to the _____. (p. 498)
    a. retirement planning process
    b. a reduction in income
    c. a sense of relief about leaving one's job or career
    d. an increase in activity

After completing the post-test, compare your score with your performance on the pre-test. Can you identify areas where significant new learning has taken place? If you still have questions about sections of the chapter, read them again. You may want to discuss some of your questions with your instructor.

Step Eight: Suggestions for Further Observation and Study

1. Explore and evaluate some web sites related to the roles acquired in grandparenthood and widowhood. Some suggested sites include:
Grandparent Times: http://www.unconnect.com/cga
Grandparents and Special Others Raising Children:
http://www.eclypse.com/GrandsRuS/grwsite.htm
National Center on Women and Aging: http://www.brandeis.edu/heller/national/ind.html

2. Further examine the "right to retirement" concept and the issue of raising the retirement age by exploring the American Association of Retired Person's web site, specifically the Raise the Retirement Age site at http://www.aarp.org/focus/ssecure/part_2/raiseage.htm.

3. What are some unique life perspectives that seem to emerge in later adulthood that help people achieve integrity? Read. E. Erikson, J. Erikson, and H. Kivnick's Vital Involvement in Old Age, New York: Norton, 1986 to help answer this question. You may also want to go to the local library and check out an autobiography. Read the autobiography and note how introspection may have helped in the writing of the autobiography. Also, note some of the other psychosocial concepts that are illustrated in the autobiography.

4. What do you think will be the special resources available to older adults in 50 years? What might be some special discoveries that will make later adulthood more psychologically satisfying? What might be some of the unique challenges to adaptation 50 years from now.

CHAPTER FOURTEEN

Very Old Age (75 until Death)

Step One: Review the Chapter Outline

The Longevity Revolution
Developmental Tasks
    Coping with the Physical Changes of Aging
        Fitness
        Behavioral Slowing
        Sensory Changes
        Health, Illness, and Functional Independence
    Developing a Psychohistorical Perspective
    Traveling Unchartered Territory: Life Structures of the Very Old
        Living Arrangements
        Gender-Role Definitions
The Psychosocial Crisis: Immortality versus Extinction
    Immortality
    Extinction
The Central Process: Social Support
    Benefits of Social Support
    The Dynamics of Social Support
The Prime Adaptive Ego Quality and the Core Pathology
    Confidence
    Diffidence
Applied Topic: Meeting the Needs of the Frail Elderly
    Defining Frailty
    Supporting Optimal Functioning
        The Role of Community
        The Role of Creative Action
Chapter Summary
End of Chapter Case

Step Two: Review the Chapter Objectives

14.1   To identify very old age as a unique developmental period for those of unusual longevity; a stage with its own developmental tasks and psychosocial crisis.

14.2   To describe some of the physical changes associated with aging, including changes in fitness, behavioral slowing, sensory changes, and vulnerability to illness, and challenges these changes pose for continued psychosocial well-being.

14.3   To develop the concept of an altered perspective on time and history that emerges among the long lived.

14.4 To identify and describe the psychosocial crisis of immortality versus extinction, the central process of social support, the prime adaptative ego quality of confidence, and the core pathology of diffidence.

14.5 To apply research and theory to concerns about meeting the needs of the frail elderly.

Step Three: Take the Pre-Test

Answer these questions before you read the text. The pages where material is discussed are indicated in the parentheses after each question. Use your performance as a guide to areas where you need to read especially carefully. The Answer Key for the pre-test can be found at the end of the study guide.

1. Approximately what percent of the population in the United States is age 75 or older who would fall under the category of very old age, according to this chapter? (p. 506)
   a. less than 1%
   b. 1%
   c. 5-10%
   d. 10-15%

2. Which of the following is NOT a developmental task associated with very old age? (p. 505)
   a. coping with physical changes of aging
   b. dealing with an organic brain disorder, such as Alzheimer's Disease
   c. developing a psychohistorical perspective
   d. traveling uncharted territory

3. Which of the following is a common characteristics of people who live a long time? (p. 507)
   a. They have few social contacts.
   b. They live an unstimulating life and do not adapt to change.
   c. They pursue activities that challenge and intrigue them.
   d. They live a life of hectic activity and high stress.

4. Which of the following statements about physical changes associated with the aging process is most accurate? (p. 509)
   a. 70-year-olds are stronger and have greater physical endurance than 30-year-olds
   b. With age, the need for calories increases.
   c. The circulatory system becomes more efficient at supplying oxygenated blood to the body with age.
   d. The strength and capacity for moderate effort in physical activities is about the same when one is 70 as when one was 40.

5. A common emotional consequence associated with vision loss is _____. (pp. 512-513)
   a. suspiciousness
   b. increased autonomy
   c. increased empathy
   d. a new sense of helplessness

6. A psychohistorical perspective refers to the ability to _____. (p. 517)
   a. remember historical events
   b. integrate information about past, present, and future
   c. anticipate the future
   d. analyze the motives of future leaders based on previous history

7. What precipitates or brings about the psychosocial crisis of immortality versus extinction? (p. 527)
   a. facing death
   b. outliving one's cohort
   c. having grandchildren
   d. feeling isolated from one's peers

8. What is one example of how social support contributes to well-being? (p.529)
   a. It reduces isolation
   b. It adds new financial obligations.
   c. It requires cognitive complexity.
   d. It increases religiosity.

9. If an older adult is unable to act because of overwhelming self doubt, the individual would be said to have _____. (p. 532)
   a. a sense of physical dependency
   b. a large social support system
   c. a sense of conscious trust in oneself
   d. a sense of diffidence

10. What is optimal functioning? (p. 534)
    a. one's achievements at age 20
    b. the best performance within a group
    c. the level of performance when a person is highly motivated and prepared
    d. the usual level of performance by an individual

Step Four: Read Chapter 14: Very Old Age

Step Five: Review the Basic Concepts By Matching Each Term and Its Definition

a. immortality
b. extinction
c. confidence
d. diffidence
e. behavioral slowing
f. psychohistorical perspective
g. social support
h. optimal ability
i. continuing care community

1. ( ) The level of performance of which one is capable at the highest level of motivation and preparation.

2. ( ) Transcendence of death through a sense of symbolic continuity.

3. ( ) Age-related delay in speed and response to stimuli.

4. ( ) A setting which offers housing, medical, preventive health, and social services as well as nursing care.

5. ( ) The inability to act as a result of overwhelming self-doubt.

6. ( ) Information leading people to believe that they are valued and part of a larger network of mutual obligation.

7. ( ) A conscious trust in oneself and in the meaningfulness of life.

8. ( ) An integration of past, present, and future time with respect to personal and societal continuity and change.

9. ( ) A sense that the end of life is the end of all continuity and connection to the future.

Step Six: Answer the Focusing Questions

1. What are the three major developmental tasks associated with very old age? (p. 505)

_____
_____
_____
_____

2. What are the challenges that behavioral slowing, sensory change, and vulnerability to illness and chronic conditions pose to individuals who are considered very old? (p. 511-515)

3. How does the formation of a psychohistorical perspective contribute to a sense of immortality? (p. 517)

4. Compare and contrast the concepts of usual aging and successful aging. (p. 519)

5. Explain the concept of sex role convergence as it pertains to males and females. (pp. 524-525)

6. What are the five ways to achieve a sense of immortality? (p. 528)

7. What are five ideas for promoting optimal functioning among frail elderly? (pp. 534-535)

Step Seven: Take the Post-Test

1. What is life endurance? (p. 507)
    a. the age to which 1 person in 100,000 can expected to live
    b. the age at which muscle strength is at its peak
    c. a measure of life satisfaction
    d. a life index of the ability to live independently

2. Age-related behavioral slowing is _____. (p. 511)
   a. more readily noticeable in routine tasks of daily living
   b. associated with simplistic tasks
   c. related to taste-smell age-related changes
   d. more readily noticeable in complex tasks

3. Which of the following sensory changes occurs in the elderly? (pp. 512-514)
   a. sharp loss in pitch discrimination
   b. inability to distinguish red from green
   c. improved distance perception
   d. improved ability to detect bitter tastes

4. Which of the following terms refers to the ability to integrate past, present, and future and to relate these concepts to patterns of continuity and change within a culture? (p. 517)
   a. optimal ability
   b. immortality
   c. psychohistorical perspective
   d. role reversal

5. Which of the following best describes sex-role convergence? (p. 524)
   a. Sex roles become more rigid and traditional.
   b. Sex roles become neutral and consistent with no change.
   c. Sex roles become more androgynous for men and women.
   d. Sex roles for men and women become more nurturant.

6. Which of the following statements about the very old is most accurate? (pp. 527-528)
   a. People with a sense of hope can cope with the reality of death better.
   b. Most people have not developed a view about death.
   c. People must cope with role gains and other accumulating processes
   d. Most people dread change at all systems levels.

7. A sense that one's life is bound by the limits of one's own life history and ends with one's death is called a sense of _____. (p. 528)
   a. existentialism
   b. limited meaningfulness
   c. finiteness
   d. extinction

Chapter 14

8. Social support contributes to well-being in three ways which include reducing isolation, providing resources, and _____. (p. 529)
   a. building endurance
   b. creating gender-role flexibility
   c. traveling unchartered territory
   d. reducing impact of stressors

9. When an adult realizes that an aging parent is no longer functioning at a high level of competence, he or she may begin to treat the parent like a child. This is an example of _____. (p. 534)
   a. filial obligation
   b. redefining the critical distance
   c. role reversal
   d. optimal performance

10. What should be the primary goal of providing services to the elderly?
    a. to enhance a realistic level of performance
    b. to get older adults to live more like 50 year olds
    c. to encourage older adults to give up their independence
    d. to relieve older adults of decision-making responsibilities.

After completing the post-test, compare your score with your performance on the pre-test. Can you identify areas where significant new learning has taken place? If you still have questions about sections of the chapter, read them again. You may want to discuss some of your questions with your instructor.

Step Eight: Suggestions for Further Observation and Study

1. Go to the web-based, Resource Directory for Older People which is a joint venture by the Administration on Aging and the National Institute on Aging at: http://www.aoa.dhhs.gov/aoa/dir/toc.html. Find a resource site for one of the chapter topics which especially interested you. Or find a resource site for a topic which you want to increase your understanding.

2. Examine your current residence or the residence of your parents using Table 14.2, Critical Distance of Neighborhood Services for the Elderly on page 535 in the text. What are some of the critical distances to various services? How many exceed the maximum recommended distance? What type of interventions can be used for those services which exceed the maximum recommended distance?

3. Visit a continuing care community and/or a nursing home. What aspects of the setting are designed to foster and maintain optimal functioning for the very old? What aspects of the setting interfere with optimal functioning?

ANSWER KEY

Chapter 1

Pre-Test				Matching				Post-Test			
1.	d	6.	a	1.	h	6.	c	1.	b	6.	b
2.	a	7.	b	2.	b	7.	j	2.	b	7.	a
3.	a	8.	d	3.	a	8.	f	3.	c	8.	b
4.	c	9.	c	4.	g	9.	e	4.	d	9.	d
5.	d	10.	a	5.	d	10.	i	5.	a	10.	c

Chapter 2

Pre-Test				Matching				Post-Test			
1.	a	6.	a	1.	b	6.	i	1.	c	6.	a
2.	b	7.	d	2.	g	7.	f	2.	a	7.	c
3.	b	8.	b	3.	j	8.	c	3.	c	8.	a
4.	c	9.	a	4.	e	9.	h	4.	d	9.	b
5.	d	10.	c	5.	d	10.	a	5.	b	10.	a

Chapter 3

Pre-Test				Matching				Post-Test			
1.	b	6.	c	1.	l	8.	f	1.	a	6.	d
2.	c	7.	d	2.	n	9.	m	2.	d	7.	a
3.	a	8.	b	3.	b	10.	h	3.	a	8.	b
4.	d	9.	a	4.	c	11.	j	4.	b	9.	d
5.	a	10.	c	5.	g	12.	d	5.	b	10.	b
				6.	a	13.	k				
				7.	e	14.	i				

Chapter 4

Pre-Test				Matching				Post-Test			
1.	d	6.	d	1.	g	7.	d	1.	b	6.	a
2.	c	7.	a	2.	c	8.	i	2.	c	7.	c
3.	a	8.	b	3.	j	9.	l	3.	a	8.	b
4.	d	9.	b	4.	a	10.	f	4.	c	9.	a
5.	b	10.	c	5.	h	11.	b	5.	d	10.	b
				6.	e	12.	k				

Chapter 5

Pre-Test				Matching				Post-Test			
1.	c	6.	c	1.	k	7.	j	1.	d	6.	d
2.	b	7.	a	2.	h	8.	i	2.	a	7.	c
3.	b	8.	a	3.	a	9.	l	3.	d	8.	b
4.	d	9.	d	4.	g	10.	b	4.	b	9.	d
5.	a	10.	b	5.	c	11.	d	5.	a	10.	b
				6.	f	12.	e				

Chapter 6

Pre-Test				Matching				Post-Test			
1.	c	6.	c	1.	b	7.	l	1.	b	6.	a
2.	a	7.	c	2.	e	8.	d	2.	d	7.	a
3.	b	8.	a	3.	h	9.	k	3.	b	8.	b
4.	d	9.	a	4.	i	10.	g	4.	c	9.	d
5.	a	10.	b	5.	a	11.	j	5.	d	10.	d
				6.	c	12.	f				

Chapter 7

Pre-Test				Matching				Post-Test			
1.	c	6.	b	1.	j	7.	f	1.	a	6.	c
2.	d	7.	c	2.	b	8.	g	2.	b	7.	d
3.	b	8.	a	3.	e	9.	h	3.	b	8.	c
4.	a	9.	d	4.	a	10.	d	4.	d	9.	a
5.	a	10.	c	5.	c	11.	l	5.	c	10.	b
				6.	i	12.	k				

Chapter 8

Pre-Test				Matching				Post-Test			
1.	b	6.	c	1.	d	7.	i	1.	b	6.	a
2.	a	7.	a	2.	j	8.	e	2.	c	7.	c
3.	d	8.	c	3.	c	9.	l	3.	c	8.	d
4.	a	9.	b	4.	a	10.	g	4.	b	9.	d
5.	c	10.	d	5.	f	11.	k	5.	c	10.	b
				6.	b	12.	h				

Chapter 9

Pre-Test				Matching				Post-Test			
1.	a	6.	c	1.	h	7.	b	1.	a	6.	c
2.	b	7.	a	2.	a	8.	c	2.	d	7.	d
3.	d	8.	b	3.	i	9.	k	3.	c	8.	c
4.	c	9.	d	4.	g	10.	f	4.	b	9.	a
5.	d	10.	c	5.	e	11.	j	5.	b	10.	b
				6.	l	12.	d				

Chapter 10

Pre-Test				Matching				Post-Test			
1.	d	6.	a	1.	c	7.	k	1.	a	6.	a
2.	c	7.	b	2.	g	8.	a	2.	b	7.	d
3.	a	8.	d	3.	h	9.	e	3.	d	8.	c
4.	a	9.	c	4.	b	10.	f	4.	d	9.	c
5.	b	10.	c	5.	d	11.	l	5.	d	10.	c
				6.	j	12.	i				

Chapter 11

Pre-Test				Matching				Post-Test			
1.	a	6.	b	1.	k	7.	f	1.	c	6.	d
2.	d	7.	a	2.	i	8.	c	2.	b	7.	b
3.	b	8.	d	3.	d	9.	l	3.	a	8.	a
4.	c	9.	b	4.	a	10.	h	4.	d	9.	a
5.	c	10.	a	5.	e	11.	g	5.	c	10.	c
				6.	b	12.	j				

Chapter 12

Pre-Test				Matching				Post-Test			
1.	c	6.	c	1.	d	6.	c	1.	d	6.	a
2.	a	7.	a	2.	h	7.	b	2.	b	7.	d
3.	c	8.	b	3.	e	8.	a	3.	c	8.	a
4.	a	9.	c	4.	i	9.	f	4.	b	9.	c
5.	c	10.	b	5.	g			5.	b	10.	b

Chapter 13

Pre-Test				Matching				Post-Test			
1.	a	6.	d	1.	k	6.	e	1.	c	6.	d
2.	c	7.	a	2.	d	7.	a	2.	b	7.	c
3.	a	8.	c	3.	g	8.	h	3.	d	8.	a
4.	c	9.	d	4.	i	9.	b	4.	d	9.	c
5.	b	10.	a	5.	f	10.	c	5.	a	10.	
						11.	j				

Chapter 14

Pre-Test				Matching				Post-Test			
1.	c	6.	b	1.	h	6.	g	1.	a	6.	a
2.	b	7.	b	2.	a	7.	c	2.	a	7.	d
3.	c	8.	a	3.	e	8.	f	3.	d	8.	d
4.	d	9.	d	4.	i	9.	b	4.	c	9.	c
5.	d	10.	c	5.	d			5.	c	10.	a

Take the guesswork out of succeeding in college with . . .

College Survival Guide:
Hints and References to Aid College Students,
Fourth Edition
by Bruce Rowe, Los Angeles Pierce College

How can I finance my college education?
Can I get credit through examination?
What can I do to get better grades on my exams?

You'll find the answers to these questions and more in Bruce Rowe's 77-page paperback. If you're like many students just starting out at college, the whole experience can be somewhat overwhelming. By the time you've figured out what you need to know to succeed, you've already wasted a lot of time and money going in wrong directions!

Now, for just $5.95*, you can get a concise guide that will give you practical information on such topics as:

- How to manage your time
- How to study for and take exams
- How to use the Internet to do research for assigned papers
- How to finance your education
- How to maintain your concentration
- How to get credit through examination
- How and when to use the credit/no credit option
- And much more!

*Download the College Survival Guide from the Internet for just $5.95!
Visit us at http://www.brookscole.com. If you do NOT have Internet access or would prefer to order by phone or mail, you can purchase the manual for $11.95 by calling toll free (800) 354-9706, or by filling out and returning the coupon provided.

ORDER FORM

Yes, I want to purchase: *College Survival Guide: Hints and References to Aid College Students, Fourth Edition* (ISBN: 0-534-35569-2)

Residents of:	AL, AZ, CA, CT, CO, FL, GA, IL, IN, KS KY, LA, MA, MD, MI, MN, MO, NC, NJ, NY, OH, PA, RI, SC, TN, TX, UT, VA, WA, WI must add appropriate state sales tax.	_____ **Copies x $11.95** _____ **Subtotal** _____ **Tax** _____ **Handling** ___**$4.00**___ **Total Due** _____	

Payment Options

_____ Check or money order enclosed *or*

Bill my _____ VISA _____ MasterCard _____ American Express

Card Number: _____

Expiration Date: _____

Signature: _____

Please ship my order to:

Name _____

Institution _____

Street Address _____

City _____ State _____ Zip+4 _____ + _____

Telephone ( ) _____

Your credit card will not be billed until your order is shipped. Prices subject to change without notice. We will refund payment for unshipped out-of-stock titles after 120 days and for not-yet-published titles after 180 days unless an earlier date is requested in writing from you.

Mail to: Wadsworth Publishing Company
Source Code 9BCPY248
Ten Davis Drive
Belmont, California 94002-3098
Phone: (800) 354-9706
Fax: (800) 522-4923

Photocopy, fold, close, and return with payment